The Doctrines and Discipline of the African Methodist Episcopal Church

A DocSouth Books Edition
The University of North Carolina at Chapel Hill Library
Chapel Hill

A DocSouth Books Edition, 2017

ISBN 978-1-4696-3325-1 (pbk.: alk. paper)

Published by
The University of North Carolina at Chapel Hill Library
CB #3900 Davis Library
Chapel Hill, NC 27514-8890
http://library.unc.edu

Documenting the American South
http://docsouth.unc.edu
docsouth@unc.edu

Distributed by
The University of North Carolina Press
116 South Boundary Street
Chapel Hill, NC 27514-3808
1-800-848-6224
http://www.uncpress.org

This book was digitally printed.

About This Edition

This edition is made available under the imprint of DocSouth Books, a collaborative endeavor between the University of North Carolina at Chapel Hill Library and the University of North Carolina Press. Titles in DocSouth Books are drawn from the Library's Documenting the American South (DocSouth) digital publishing program, online at docsouth.unc.edu. These print and downloadable e-book editions have been prepared from the DocSouth electronic editions.

Both DocSouth and DocSouth Books present the transcribed content of historic books as they were originally published. Grammar, punctuation, spelling, and typographical errors are therefore preserved from the original editions. DocSouth Books are not intended to be facsimile editions, however. Details of typography and page layout in the original works have not been preserved in the transcription.

DocSouth Books editions incorporate two pagination schemas. First, standard page numbers reflecting the pagination of this edition appear at the top of each page for easy reference. Second, page numbers in brackets within the text (e.g., "[Page 9]") refer to the pagination of the original publication; online versions of the DocSouth works use this same original pagination. Page numbers shown in tables of contents and book indexes, when present, refer to the original works' printed page numbers and therefore correspond to the page numbers in brackets.

Summary

Published in 1817, *The Doctrines and Discipline of the African Methodist Episcopal Church* was the first Discipline published by the African Methodist Episcopal (A.M.E.) Church. "Discipline" here can be thought of in one of the registers offered by the Oxford English Dictionary: "instruction as given to disciples, scholars, etc.; schooling, teaching." It is a slim but definitive guide to the history, beliefs, teachings, and practices of the early A.M.E. Church. It begins with a brief history of that Church, and moves into a presentation of the "Articles of Religion," including: the Trinity, the Word of God, scripture, original sin and free will, works, sacraments, baptism, Lord's Supper, church ceremonies, and government. Some of the articles in this first section are quite specific, for example, the rejection of speaking in tongues in church. Immediately following the articles is an extended four-part catechism that more fully explicates the meanings and implications of the doctrinal statements.

The rest of the document is concerned with the practical matters of denominational organization. It gives guidelines for the composition and agenda of the "General Conference" and "Yearly Conferences," specific qualifications and duties of superintendents, elders, and preachers, along with advice for the education of children. The book also takes up various kinds of "united societies," providing both guidelines for duty and pitfalls to be avoided in class meetings and band societies. Proper practice and beliefs concerning marriage, dress, and liquor are covered, apparently in response to controversies at the time of its writing.

Instructions for sacramental services follow, and the book provides scripture, text, prayer, and order of service for "Lord's Supper," baptisms, weddings, funerals, and ordinations. The final section of the book considers concerns of the moment, a "Temporal Economy" that provides guidelines for preachers' salaries, fundraising for home missions, the operation of a publishing venture (the A.M.E.'s Book Concern) and the proscription of slaveholders in the A.M.E. Church.

Christopher Hill

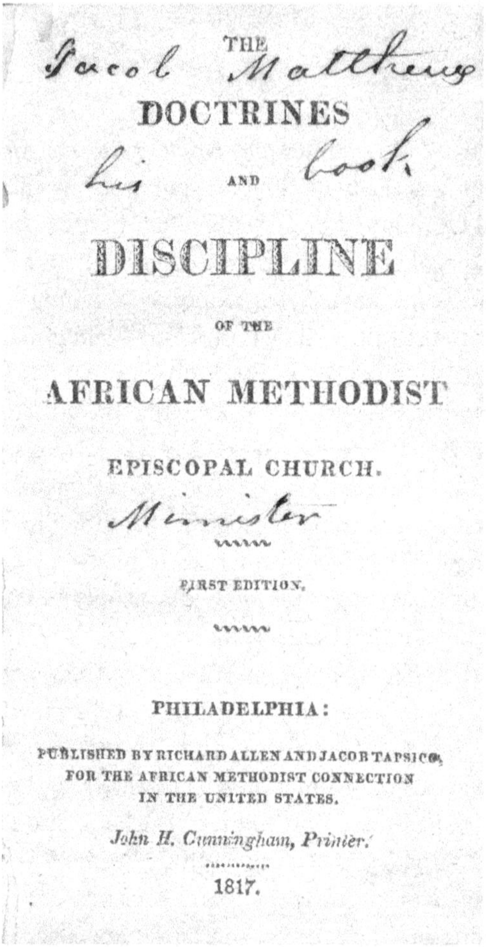

Jacob Matthews

THE

DOCTRINES

his AND book.

DISCIPLINE

OF THE

AFRICAN METHODIST

EPISCOPAL CHURCH.

Minister

FIRST EDITION.

PHILADELPHIA:

PUBLISHED BY RICHARD ALLEN AND JACOB TAPSICO,
FOR THE AFRICAN METHODIST CONNECTION
IN THE UNITED STATES.

John H. Cunningham, Printer.

1817.

[Title Page Image]

THE DOCTRINES AND DISCIPLINE OF THE AFRICAN METHODIST EPISCOPAL CHURCH.

FIRST EDITION.
PHILADELPHIA:
PUBLISHED BY RICHARD ALLEN AND JACOB TAPSICO
FOR THE AFRICAN METHODIST CONNECTION
IN THE UNITED STATES.
John H. Cunningham, Printer.
1817.

[Page 3] TO THE MEMBERS OF THE AFRICAN METHODIST EPISCOPAL CHURCH, IN THE UNITED STATES OF AMERICA:

Beloved Brethren,

We deem it necessary to annex to our book of discipline, a brief statement of our rise and progress, which we hope will be satisfactory, and conducive to your edification and growth in the knowledge of our Lord Jesus Christ. In November, 1787, the coloured people belonging to the Methodist Society in Philadelphia, convened together, in order to take into consideration the evils under which they laboured, arising from the unkind treatment of their white brethren, who considered them a nuisance in the house of worship, and even pulled them off their knees while in the act of prayer, and ordered them to the back seats. From these, and various other acts of unchristian conduct, we considered it our duty to devise a plan in order to build a house of our own, to worship God under our own vine and fig tree: in this undertaking, we met with great opposition from an elder of the Methodist church (J. McC.) who threatened, that if we did not give up the building, erase our names from the subscription paper, and make acknowledgments for having attempted such a thing, that in three months we should all be publicly expelled from the Methodist society. Not considering ourselves bound to obey this injunction, and being fully satisfied we should be treated without mercy, we sent in our resignations.

[Page 4]Being now as outcasts, we had to seek for friends where we could; and the Lord put it into the hearts of Dr. Benjamin Rush, Mr. R. Ralston, and other respectable citizens, to interpose for us, both by advice and assistance, in getting our building finished: Bishop White also aided us, and ordained one from among ourselves, after the order of the English church, to be our pastor.

In 1793, the number of serious people of colour, being greatly increased, they were of different opinions respecting the mode of religious worship; and, as many felt a strong partiality for that adopted by the Methodists, Richard Allen, with the advice of some of his brethren, proposed erecting a place of worship on his own ground, and at his own expense, as an African Methodist Meetinghouse. As soon as the preachers of the white Methodist church, in Philadelphia, came to the knowledge of this, they opposed it with all their might, insisting that the house should be made over to the conference, or they would publish us in the newspapers as imposing on the public, as we were not Methodists. However, the building went on, and when finished, we invited Francis Asbury, then bishop of the Methodist Episcopal Church, to open the house for Divine service; which invitation he accepted, and the house was named BETHEL. (See Gen. chap. 28)

It was now proposed by the resident elder, (J. McC.) that we should have the Church incorporated, that we might receive any donation or legacy, as well as enjoy other advantages arising therefrom. This was agreed to; and, in order to save expense, the elder [Page 5] proposed drawing it up for us. But, we soon found he had done it in such a manner as entirely deprived us of that liberty we expected to enjoy. So that by this stratagem, we were again brought into bondage by the white preachers.

In this situation, we experienced grievances too numerous to mention: at one time, the elder (J.S.) demanded the keys of the house, with the books and papers belonging to the church; telling us at other times, we should have no more meetings without his leave—and, that the house was not ours, but belonged to the Methodist conference. Finding ourselves thus embarrassed, we consulted a lawyer, who informed us that by means of a supplement, we could be delivered from the grievances we laboured under. The congregation were unanimous, in signing the petition for a supplement, which the legislature of Pennsylvania readily granted; and we were liberated from the difficulties which, for ten years, we experienced. We now hoped to be free from any further perplexity; but we soon found, that our proceedings respecting the supplement, exasperated our opponents. In order to accommodate matters, they proposed supplying us with preaching, if we would give them $600 per year. The congregation not consenting to this sum, they fell to $400; but the people were not willing to give more than $200 per year. For which sum, they were to preach for us twice a week, during the year. But it proved to be only six or seven times; and sometimes by such preachers as were not acceptable to the Bethel people, and not in much esteem among [Page 6] the white Methodists, as preachers. The Bethel people being dissatisfied with such conduct, induced the trustees to pass a resolution to give but $100 per year, to the white ministers. When a quarterly payment of the $100 was tendered, it was refused, and sent back, insisting on the $200, or we should have no more preaching from them. At this time they strongly pressed us to repeal the supplement; this we could not comply with.

We waited on bishop Asbury, and proposed taking a preacher to ourselves, and supporting him in boarding and salary, provided he would attend to the duties of the church; such as, visiting the sick, burying the dead, baptising, and administering the sacrament. The bishop observed, "He did not think there was more than one preacher belonging to the conference who would attend to those duties." It was then asked, "Who was to do the duties?" the bishop answered, "You," referring to Richard Allen. The bishop being informed that if we paid a preacher four or five hundred dollars per year, we should expect that preacher to do his duty, replied, that "We would not be served on them terms."

Shortly after this, an elder (S. R.) then in Philadelphia, declared that unless we would repeal the supplement, neither he nor any white preacher, travelling or local, should preach any more for us: so we were left to ourselves. At length, the preachers and stewards belonging to the Academy, proposed serving us on the same terms that we had offered to the St. George's preachers: and they preached for us better than twelve months, and then demanded $150 per year; [Page 7] this not being complied with, they declined preaching for us, and we were once more left to ourselves, as an edict was passed by the elder, that if any local preacher should serve us, he should be expelled the connection. John Emory, then elder of the Academy, published a circular letter, in which we were disowned by the Methodists.—A house was also hired, and fitted up for worship, not far from Bethel, and an invitation given to all who desired to be Methodists, to resort thither. But being disappointed in this plan, Robert R. Roberts, the resident elder, came to Bethel, insisted on preaching to us, and taking the spiritual charge of the congregation, for we were Methodists. He was told he should come on some terms with the trustees; his answer was, that "He did not come to consult with Richard Allen, or other trustees, but to inform the congregation, that on next Sunday afternoon, he would come and take the spiritual charge." We told him "He could not preach for us under existing circumstances." However, at the appointed time, he came; but having taken previous advice, we had our preacher in the pulpit when he came, and the house so fixt, that he could not get more than half way to the pulpit—finding himself disappointed, he appealed to those who came with him as witnesses, that "That man (meaning the preacher) had taken his appointment." Several respectable white citizens, who knew the coloured people had been ill used, were present, and told us not to fear, for they would see us righted, and not suffer Roberts to preach in a forcible manner: after which Roberts went away.

[Page 8] The next elder stationed in Philadelphia, was Robert Birch, who, following the example of his predecessor, came and published a meeting for himself; but the method just mentioned, was adopted, and he had to go away disappointed. In consequence of this, he applied to the supreme court for a writ of *Mandamus,* to know why the pulpit was denied him, being elder: this brought on a law suit, which ended in our favour. Thus, by the providence of God, we were delivered from a long, distressing, and expensive suit, which could not be resumed, being determined by the supreme court: for this mercy we desire to be unfeignedly thankful.

About this time, our coloured friends at Baltimore, were treated in a similar manner, by the white preachers and trustees, and many of them drove away; who were disposed to seek a place of worship for themselves, rather than go to law.

Many of the coloured people, in other places, were in a situation nearly like those of Philadelphia and Baltimore, which induced us, last April, to call a general meeting, by way of conference. Delegates from Baltimore, and other places, met those of Philadelphia, and taking into consideration their grievances, and in order to secure their privileges, promote union and harmony among themselves, it was resolved, "That the people of Philadelphia, Baltimore, &c. &c. should become one body, under the name of the African Methodist Episcopal Church." We have deemed it expedient to have a form of Discipline, whereby we may guide our people in the fear of God, in the unity of the Spirit, and [Page 9] in the bonds of peace, and preserve us from that spiritual despotism which we have so recently experienced—remembering, that we are not to Lord it over God's heritage, as greedy dogs, that can never have enough; but with long suffering, and bowels of compassion, to bear each other's burthens, and so fulfil the law of Christ; praying that our mutual striving together, for the promulgation of the gospel, may be crowned with abundant success, we remain your affectionate servants in the kingdom and patience of the Prince of Peace.

RICHARD ALLEN, DANIEL COKER,
JAMES CHAMPION.

[Page 10] *Proceeding of the Convention.*

On the 11th April, 1816, RICHARD ALLEN was solemnly set apart for the Episcopal Office, by prayer and the imposition of the hands of five regularly ordained ministers. At which time, the General Convention held in Philadelphia, did unanimously receive the said Richard Allen as their bishop, being fully satisfied of the validity of his Episcopal Ordination.

DOCTRINES AND DISCIPLINE OF THE AFRICAN METHODIST EPISCOPAL CHURCH.

CHAPTER I.

SECTION I.

ARTICLES OF RELIGION.

I. *Of Faith in the Holy Trinity.*

THERE is but one living and true God, everlasting, without body or parts, of infinite power, wisdom, and goodness: the maker and preserver of all things, both visible and invisible. And in unity of this God-head, there are three persons of one substance, power and eternity;—the Father, the Son, and the Holy Ghost.

II. *Of the Word, or Son of God, who was made very Man.*

THE Son, who is the Word of the Father, the very and eternal God, of [Page 12] one substance with the Father, took man's nature in the womb of the blessed Virgin; so that two whole and perfect natures, that is to say, the God-head and manhood, were joined together in one person, never to be divided, whereof is one Christ, very God and very man, who truly suffered, was crucified, dead and buried, to reconcile his Father to us, and to be a sacrifice, not only for original guilt, but also for actual sins of men.

III. *Of the Resurrection of Christ.*

CHRIST did truly rise again from the dead, and took again his body with all things appertaining to the perfection of man's nature, where-with he ascended into heaven, and there sitteth until he return to judge all men at the last day.

IV. *Of the Holy Ghost.*

THE Holy Ghost, proceeding from the Father and the Son, is of one substance, majesty, and glory with the Father and the Son, very and eternal God.

[Page 13] V. *The Sufficiency of the Holy Scripture for Salvation.*

HOLY Scripture containeth all things necessary to salvation: so that whatsoever is not read therein, nor may be proved thereby, is not to be required of any man, that it should be believed as an article of faith, or be thought requisite or necessary to salvation. In the name of the Holy Scripture, we do understand those canonical books of the Old and New Testament, of whose authority was never any doubt in the church.

The Names of the Canonical Books.

GENESIS,
Exodus,
Leviticus,
Numbers,
Deuteronomy,
Joshua,
Judges,
Ruth,
The First Book of Samuel,
The Second Book of Samuel,
The First Book of Kings,
The Second Book of Kings,
[Page 14]The First Book of Chronicles,
The Second Book of Chronicles,
The Book of Ezra,
The Book of Nehemiah,
The Book of Esther,

The Book of Job,
The Psalms,
The Proverbs,
Ecclesiastes, or the Preacher,
Cantica, or Songs of Solomon,
Four Prophets the greater,
Twelve Prophets the less:

All the Books of the New Testament as they are commonly received, we do receive and account canonical.

VI. *Of the Old Testament.*

THE Old Testament is not contrary to the New: for both in the Old and New Testament, everlasting life is offered to mankind by Christ, who is the only Mediator between God and man, being both God and man. Wherefore they are not to be heard, who feign that the old Fathers did look only for transitory promises. Although the law given from God [Page 15] by Moses, as touching ceremonies and rites, doth not bind Christians, nor ought the civil precepts thereof of necessity be received in any commonwealth: yet, notwithstanding, no christian whatsoever is free from the obedience of the commandments, which are called moral.

VII. *Of Original or Birth Sin.*

ORIGINAL sin standeth not in the following of Adam (as the Pelagians do vainly talk) but it is the corruption of the nature of every man, that naturally is engendered of the offspring of Adam, whereby man is very far gone from original righteousness, and of his own nature inclined to evil, and that continually.

VIII. *Of Free-Will.*

THE condition of man after the fall of Adam is such, that he cannot turn and prepare himself by his own natural strength and works to faith, and calling upon God: Wherefore we have no power to do good works, without the grace of God by Christ [Page 16] preventing us, that we may have a good will, and working with us, when we have that good will.

IX. *Of the Justification of Man.*

WE are accounted righteous before God, only for the merit of our Lord and Saviour Jesus Christ by faith, and not for our own works or deservings;—Wherefore, that we are justified by faith, only, is a most wholesome doctrine, and very full of comfort.

X. *Of Good Works.*

ALTHOUGH good works, which are the fruits of faith, and follow after justification, cannot put away our sins, and endure the severity of God's judgments: yet are they pleasing and acceptable to God in Christ, and spring out of a true and lively faith, insomuch that by them a lively faith may be as evidently known, as a tree is discerned by its fruit.

XI. *Of Works of Supererogation.*

VOLUNTARY works, besides, over and above God's commandments, [Page 17] which they call works of supererogation, cannot be taught without arrogancy and impiety. For by them men do declare, That they do not only render unto God as much as they are bound to do, but that they do more for his sake than of bounden duty is required: Whereas Christ saith plainly, When ye have done all that is commanded you, say, We are unprofitable servants.

XII. *Of Sin after Justification.*

NOT every sin willingly committed after justification, is the sin against the Holy Ghost, and unpardonable. Wherefore the grant of repentance is not to be denied to such as fall into sin after justification: After we have received the Holy Ghost, we may depart from grace given, and fall into sin, and by the grace of God, rise again, and amend our lives. And therefore they are to be condemned, who say they can no more sin as long as they live here; or deny the place of forgiveness to such as truly repent.

[Page 18] *XIII. Of the Church.*

THE visible Church of Christ is a congregation of faithful men, in which the pure word of God is preached, and the sacraments duly administered according to Christ's ordinance, in all those things that of necessity are requisite to the same.

XIV. *Of Purgatory.*

THE Romish doctrine concerning purgatory, pardon, worshipping, and adoration, as well of images as of relics, and also invocations of saints, is a fond thing vainly invented, and grounded upon no warrant of scripture, but repugnant to the word of God.

XV. *Of speaking in the Congregation in such a Tongue as the People understand.*

IT is a thing plainly repugnant to the word of God, and the custom of the primitive church, to have public prayer in the church, or to minister the sacraments, in a tongue not understood by the people.

[Page 19] XVI. *Of the Sacraments.*

SACRAMENTS ordained of Christ, are not only badges or tokens of Christian men's profession: but rather they are certain signs of grace, and God's good will towards us, by the which he doth work invisibly in us, and doth not only quicken, but also, strengthen and confirm our faith in him.

There are two sacraments ordained of Christ our Lord, in the gospel; that is to say, Baptism and the Supper of the Lord.

Those five commonly called sacraments; that is to say, Confirmation, Penance, Orders, Matrimony, and extreme Unction, are not to be counted for Sacraments of the Gospel, being such as have partly grown out of the *corrupt* following of the Apostles; and partly are states of life allowed in the Scriptures, but yet have not the like nature of Baptism and the Lord's Supper, because they have not any visible sign, or ceremony ordained of God.

The Sacraments were not ordained [Page 20] of Christ to be gazed upon, or to be carried about; but that we should duly use them. And in such only as worthily receive the same, they have a wholesome effect or operation; but they that receive them unworthily, purchase to themselves condemnation, as St. Paul saith.

XVII. *Of Baptism.*

BAPTISM is not only a sign of profession, and mark of difference, whereby Christians are distisguished from others that are not baptised; but it is also a sign of regeneration, or the new birth. The baptism of young children is to be retained in the church.

XVIII. *Of the Lord's Supper.*

THE Supper of the Lord is not only a sign of the love that Christians ought to have among themselves one to another, but rather is a sacrament of our redmeption by Christ's death: insomuch, that to such as rightly, worthily, and with faith receive the same, the bread which we break is a [Page 21] partaking of the body of Christ; and likewise the cup of blessing, is a partaking of the blood of Christ.

Transubstantiation, or the change of the substance of bread and wine in the Supper of our Lord, cannot be proved by Holy Writ; but is repugnant to the plain words of Scripture, overthroweth the nature of a sacrament, and hath given occasion to many superstitions.

The body of Christ is given, taken, and eaten, in the Supper, only after a heavenly and scriptural manner.— And the mean whereby the body of Christ is received and eaten in the Supper, is faith.

The Sacrament of the Lord's Supper was not by Christ's ordinance, reserved, carried about, lifted up, or worshipped.

XIX. *Of both kinds.*

THE cup of the Lord is not to be denied to the lay people: for both the parts of the Lord's Supper, by Christ's ordinance and commandment, ought to be administered to all Christians alike.

[Page 22] XX. *Of the one oblation of Christ, finished upon the Cross.*

THE offering of Christ once made, is that perfect redemption, propitiation, and satisfaction, for all the sins of the whole world, both original and actual: and there is none other satisfaction for sin but that alone. Wherefore the sacrifice of masses, in the which it is commonly said that the priest doth offer Christ for the quick and the dead, to have remission of pain or guilt, is a blasphemous fable, and dangerous deceit.

XXI. *Of the Marriage of Ministers.*

THE ministers of Christ are not commanded by God's law either to vow the estate of single life, or to abstain from marriage; therefore, it is lawful for them, as for all other Christians, to marry at their own discretion, as they shall judge the same to serve best to Godliness.

XXII. *Of the Rites and Ceremonies of Churches.*

IT is not necessary that rites and [Page 23] ceremonies should in all places be the same, or exactly alike: for they have been always different, and may be changed according to the diversity of countries, times, and men's manners, so that nothing be ordained against God's word.—Whosoever, through his private judgment, willingly and purposely, doth openly break the rites and ceremonies of the church to which he belongs, which are not repugnant to the word of God, and are ordained and approved by common authority, ought to be rebuked openly, that others may fear to do the like, as one that offendeth against the common order of the church, and woundeth the consciences of weak brethren.

Every particular church may ordain, change, or abolish, rites and ceremonies, so that all things may be done to edification.

XXIII. *Of the Rulers of the United States of America.*

THE president, the congress, the general assemblies, the governors, [Page 24] and the councils of state, *as the delegates of the people,* are the rulers of the United States of America, according to the division of power made to them by the constitution of the United States, and by the constitutions of their respective states. And the said states are a sovereign and independent nation, and ought not to be subject to any foreign jurisdiction.

XXIV. *Of Christian. Men's Goods.*

THE riches and goods of Christians are not common as touching the right, title, and possession of the same, as some do falsely boast. Notwithstanding, every man ought, of such things as he possesseth, liberally to give alms to the poor, according to his ability.

XXV. *Of a Christian Man's Oath.*

As we confess that vain and rash swearing is forbidden Christian men by our Lord Jesus Christ and James his apostle; so we judge, that the Christian religion doth not prohibit, but that a man may swear when the [Page 25] magistrate requireth, in a cause of faith and charity, so it be done according to the prophet's teaching, in justice, judgment, and truth.

SECTION II.

I. *Quest.* 1. What is it to be justified?

Answ. To be pardoned and received into God's favour; into such a state, that if we continue therein, we shall be finally saved.

Q. 2. Is faith the condition of justification?

A. Yes, for every one who believeth not is condemned; and every one who believes is justified.

Q. 3. But must not repentance, and works meet for repentance, go before this faith?

A. Without doubt: if by repentance you mean conviction of sin; and by works meet for repentance, obeying God as far as we can, forgiving our brother, leaving off from evil, doing good and using his ordinances according to the power we have received.

Q. 4. What is faith?

[Page 26]A. Faith in general is a divine supernatural *elenchos* of things not seen; *i. e.* of past, future or spiritual things; it is a spiritual view of God and the things of God.

First, a sinner is convinced by the Holy Ghost, Christ loved me, and gave himself for me.—This is that faith by which he is justified or pardoned, the moment he receives it. Immediately the same spirit bears witness, Thou art pardoned; thou hast redemption in his blood!—And this is saving faith, whereby the love of God is shed abroad in his heart.

Q. 5. Have all Christians this faith? May not a man be justified and not know it?

A. That all true Christians have such a faith as implies an assurance of God's love, appears from *Rom.* viii. 15. *Eph.* iv. 32. 2 *Cor.* xiii. 5. *Heb.* viii. 10. 1 *John* iv. 10. v. 19. And that no man can be justified and not know it, appears further from the nature of the thing: For, faith after repentance, is ease after pain, rest after toil, light after darkness. It appears also from the immediate, [Page 27] as well as distant, fruits thereof.

Q. 6. But may not a man go to heaven without it?

A. It does not appear from holy writ that a man who has heard the gospel can: (*Mark* xvi. 16.) whatever a heathen may do. *Rom.* ii. 14.

Q. 7. What are the immediate fruits of justifying faith?

A. Peace, joy, love, power over all outward sin, and power to keep down inward sin.

Q. 8. Does any one believe, who has not the witness in himself, or any longer than he sees, loves, and obeys God?

A. We apprehend not, *seeing* God being the very essence of faith; love and obedience being the inseparable properties of it.

Q. 9. What sins are consistent with justifying faith?

A. No wilful sin. If a believer *wilfully sins,* he casts away his faith. Neither is it possible he should have justifying faith again, without previously repenting.

Q. 10. *Must* every believer come [Page 28] into a state of doubt or fear, or darkness? Will he do so, unless by ignorance or unfaithfulness? Does God otherwise withdraw himself?

A. It is certain, a believer, *need* never again come into condemnation. It seems, he need not come into a state of doubt or fear, or darkness; and that (ordinarily at least) he *will* not, unless by ignorance or unfaithfulness. Yet it is true, that the first joy does seldom last long: that it is followed by doubts and fears; and that God frequently permits great heaviness, before any large manifestation of himself.

Q. 11. Are works necessary to the continuance of faith?

A. Without doubt; for a man may forfeit the free gift of God, either by sins of omission or commission.

Q. 12. Can faith be lost, but for want of works?

A. It cannot but through disobedience.

Q. 13. How is faith *made perfect by works?*

A. The more we exert our faith the more it is increased. To him that hath shall be given.

[Page 29]*Q.* 14. St. *Paul* says, *Abraham* was *not justified by works; St. James,* he was *justified by works.* Do they not contradict each other?

A. No: 1st. Because they do not speak of the same justification. *St. Paul* speaks of that justification which was when *Abraham* was seventy-five years old, above twenty years before *Isaac* was born. *St. James* of that justification which was when he offered up *Isaac* on the altar.

2d. Because they do not speak of the same works: *St. Paul* speaking of works that precede faith; *St. James* of works that spring from it.

Q. 15. In what sense is *Adam's* sin imputed to all mankind?

A. In *Adam* all die, *i. e.* 1st. Our bodies then became mortal. 2d. Our souls died, *i. e.* were disunited from God. And hence, 3d. We are all born with a sinful devilish nature: by reason whereof, 4th. We are children of wrath, liable to death eternal. *Rom.* v. 18. *Eph.* ii. 3.

Q. 16. In what sense is the righteousness of Christ imputed to all mankind, or to believers?

[Page 30]A. We do not find it expressly affirmed in scripture, that God imputes the righteousness of Christ to any. Although we do find, that faith is imputed to us for righteousness.

That text, *As by one man's disobedience all men were made sinners, so by the obedience of one, all were made righteous,* we conceive means, by the merits of Christ, all men are cleared from the guilt of *Adam's* actual sin.

We conceive further, That through the obedience and death of *Christ,* 1st. The bodies of all men become immortal after the resurrection. 2d. Their souls receive a capacity of spiritual life; and, 3d. An actual spark or seed thereof. 4th. All believers become children of grace, reconciled to God, and 5th. made partakers of the divine nature.

Q. 17. Have we not then unawares leaned too much towards *Calvinism?*

A. We are afraid we have.

Q. 18. Have we not also leaned towards *Antinomianism?*

A. We are afraid we have.

Q. 19. What is *Antinomianism?*

A. The doctrine which makes void the law through faith.

[Page 31]Q. 20. What are the main pillars hereof?

A. 1st. That Christ abolished the moral law. 2d. That therefore Christians are not obliged to observe it. 3d. That one branch of Christian liberty, is liberty from obeying the commandments of God. 4th. That it is bondage, to do a thing, because it is commannded, or forbear it because it is forbidden. 5th. That a believer is not *obliged* to use the ordinances of God or to do good works. 6th. That a preacher ought not to exhort to good works: not unbelievers, because it is hurtful; not believers, because it is needless.

Q. 21. What was the occasion of *St. Paul's* writing his epistle to the *Galatians?*

A. The coming of certain men amongst the *Galatians,* who taught, *except ye be circumcised and keep the law of* Moses *ye cannot be saved.*

Q. 22. What is his main design therein?

A. To prove, 1st. That no man can be justified or saved by the works of the law, either moral or ritual. 2d. [Page 32] That every believer is justified by faith in *Christ,* without the works of the law.

Q. 23. What does he mean by the *Works of the law? Gal.* ii. 16, &c.

A. All works which do not spring from faith in *Christ.*

Q. 24. What by being *under the law. Gal.* iii. 23?

A. Under the *Mosaic* dispensation.

Q. 25. What law has *Christ* abolished?

A. The ritual law of *Moses.*

Q. 26. What is meant by *liberty? Gal.* v. 1.

A. Liberty, 1st. From the law; 2d. From sin?

II. Q. 1st. How comes what is written on this subject* to be so intricate and obscure? Is this obscurity from the nature of the thing itself? Or, from the fault or weakness of those who have generally treated of it? A. We apprehend this obscurity does not arise from the nature of the subject: but partly from the extreme warmth of most writers who have treated of it.

[Page 33] Q. 2. We affirm faith in *Christ* is the sole condition of justification. But does not repentance go before that faith? Yea, and (supposing there be opportunity for them) fruits or works meet for repentance?

A. Without doubt they do.

Q. 3. How then can we deny them to be *conditions* of justification? Is not this a mere strife of words?

A. It seems not, though it has been grievously abused. But so the abuse cease, let the use remain.

Q. 4. Shall we read over together, *Mr. Baxter's* aphorisms concerning justification?

A. By all means: which were accordingly read. And it was desired, that each person present would in the afternoon consult the scriptures cited therein, and bring what objections might occur the next morning.

Q. 5. Is an assurance of God's pardoning love absolutely necessary to our being in his favour? Or may there possibly be some exempt cases?

A. We dare not positively say there are not.

---

* On Justification.

Q. 6. Is such an assurance absolutely [Page 34] necessary to inward and outward holiness?

A. To inward we apprehend it is: to outward holiness we incline to think it is not.

Q. 7. Is it indispensably necessary to final salvation?

A. Love hopeth all things. We know not how far any may fall under the case of invincible ignorance.

Q. 8. But what can we say of one of our own society, who dies without it, as J. W. at London?

A. It may possibly be an exempt case (if the fact was really so.) But we determine nothing. We leave his soul in the hands of him that made it.

Q. 9. Does a man believe any longer than he sees a reconciled God?

A. We conceive not. But we allow there may be infinite degrees in seeing God: even as many as there are between him that sees the sun, when it shines on his eye-lids closed, and him who stands with his eyes wide open in the full blaze of his beams.

Q. 10. Does a man believe any longer than he loves God?

A. In no wise. For neither circumcision [Page 35] or uncircumcision avails, without faith working by love.

Q. 11. Have we duly considered the case of *Cornelius?* Was not he in the favour of God *when his prayers and alms came up for a memorial before God? i. e.* before he believed in *Christ?*

A. It does seem that he was, in some degree. But we speak not of those who have not heard the gospel.

Q. 12. But were those works of his *splendid sins?*

A. No; nor were they *done without the grace of* Christ.

Q. 13. How then can we maintain, that all works done before we have a sense of the pardoning love of God, are sin? And, as such, an abomination to him?

A. The works of him who has heard the gospel, and does not believe, are not done as God hath *willed and commanded them to be done.* And yet we know not how to say, that they are an abomination to the Lord in him who feareth God, and from that principle does the best he can.

Q. 14. Seeing there is so much difficulty [Page 36] in this subject, can we deal too tenderly with them that oppose us?

A. We cannot; unless we were to give up any part of the truth of God.

Q. 15. Is a believer *constrained* to obey God?

A. At first he often is. The love of *Christ* constraineth him. After this, he may obey, or he may not; no constraint being laid upon him.

Q. 16. Can faith be lost but through disobedience?

A. It cannot. A believer first inwardly disobeys, inclines to sin with his heart: then his intercourse with God is cut off, *i. e.* his faith is lost. And after this he may fall into outward sin, being now weak, and like another man.

Q. 17. How can such an one recover faith?

A. By repenting and doing the first works. *Rev.* ii. 5.

Q. 18. Whence is it that so great a majority of those who believe, fall more or less into doubt or fear?

A. Chiefly from their own ignorance or unfaithfulness: often from [Page 37] their not watching unto prayer: perhaps from some defect or want of the power of God in the preaching they hear.

Q. 19. Is there not a defect in us? Do we preach as we did at first? Have we not changed our doctrines?

A. 1st. At first we preached almost wholly to unbelievers. To those therefore we spake almost continually, of remission of sins through the death of Christ, and the nature of faith in his blood. And so we do still, among those who need to be taught the first elements of the gospel of Christ.

2d. But those in whom the foundation is already laid, we exhort to go on to perfection: which we did not see so clearly at first; although we occasionally spoke of it from the beginning.

3d. Yet we now preach, and that continually, faith in Christ, as the prophet, priest, and king, at least, as clearly, as strongly, and as fully, as we did six years ago.

Q. 20. Do not some of our assistants preach too much of the wrath, and too little of the love of God?

[Page 38]A. We fear they have leaned to that extreme; and hence some of their hearers may have lost the joy of faith.

Q. 21. Need we ever preach the terrors of the Lord to those who know they are accepted of him?

A. No; it is folly so to do: for love is to them the strongest of all motives.

Q. 22. Do we ordinarily represent a justified state so great and happy as it is?

A. Perhaps not. A believer walking in the light, is inexpressibly great and happy.

Q. 23. Should we not have a care of depreciating justification, in order to exalt the state of full sanctification?

A. Undoubtedly we should beware of this: for one may insensibly slide into it.

Q. 24. How shall we effectually avoid it?

A. When we are going to speak of entire sanctification, let us first describe the blessings of a justified state as strongly as possible.

Q. 25. Does not the truth of the [Page 39] gospel lie very near both to *Calvinism* and *Antinomianism*?

A. Indeed it does: as it were within a hair's breadth. So that it is altogether foolish and sinful, because we do not altogether agree either with one or the other, to run from them as far as ever we can.

Q. 26. Wherein may we come to the very edge of *Calvinism*?

A. 1st. In ascribing all good to the free grace of God: 2d. In denying all natural free will, and all power antecedent to grace; and, 3d. In excluding all merit from man; even for what he has or does by the grace of God.

Q. 27. Wherein may we come to the edge of *Antinomianism*?

A. 1st. In exalting the merits and love of *Christ*. 2d. In rejoicing evermore.

Q. 28. Does faith supersede (set aside the necessity of) holiness or good works?

A. In no wise. So far from it that it implies both, as a cause does its effects?

[Page 40]III. Q. 1. Can an unbeliever (whatever he be in other respects) challenge any thing of God's justice?

A. Absolutely nothing but hell. And this is a point which we cannot too much insist on.

Q. 2. Do we empty men of their own righteousness, as we did at first? Do we sufficiently labour, when they begin to be convinced of sin, to take away all they lean upon? Should we not then endeavour with all our might to overturn their false foundations?

A. This was at first one of our principal points. And it ought to be so still. For, till all other foundations are overturned, they cannot build upon Christ.

Q. 3. Did we not *then* purposely throw them into convictions? Into strong sorrow and fear? Nay, did we not strive to make them inconsolable? Refusing to be comforted?

A. We did. And so we should do still. For the stronger the conviction, the speedier is the deliverance. And none so soon receive the peace of God, as those who steadily refuse all other comfort.

[Page 41]*Q.* 4. What is sincerity?

A. Willingness to know and do the whole will of God. The lowest species thereof seems to be *faithfulness in that which is little.*

Q. 5. Has God any regard to man's sincerity?

A. So far, that no man in any state can possibly please God without it: neither indeed in any moment wherein he is not sincere.

Q. 6. But can it be conceived that God has any regard to the sincerity of an unbeliever?

A. Yes, so much, that if he perseveres therein, God will infallibly give him faith.

Q. 7. What regard may we conceive him to have, to the sincerity of a believer?

A. So much, that in every sincere believer he fulfils all the great and precious promises.

Q. 8. Whom do you term a *sincere believer?*

A. One that walks in the light, as God is in the light.

Q. 9. Is sincerity the same with a *single eye?*

[Page 42]*A.* Not altogether: the latter refers to our intention; the former to our will or desires.

Q. 10. Is it not all in all?

A. All will follow persevering sincerity. God gives every thing with it; nothing without it.

Q. 11. Are not then sincerity and faith equivalent terms?

A. By no means. It is at least as nearly related to works as it is to faith. For example: Who is sincere before he believes? He that then does all he can: he that, according to the power he has received, brings forth *fruits meet for repentance.* Who is sincere after he believes? He that, from a sense of God's love, is zealous of all good works.

Q. 12. Is not sincerity what *St. Paul* terms a willing mind? 2 *Cor.* viii. 12.

A. Yes: if that word be taken in a general sense. For it is a constant disposition to use all the grace given.

Q. 13. But do we not then set sincerity on a level with faith?

A. No: For we allow a man may be sincere, and not be justified, as he may be penitent, and not be justified: [Page 43] (not as yet) but he cannot have faith, and not be justified. The very moment he believes he is justified.

Q. 14. But do we not give up faith, and put sincerity in its place, as the condition of our acceptance with God?

A. We believe it is one condition of our acceptance, as repentance likewise is. And we believe it a condition of our continuing in a state of acceptance. Yet we do not put it in the place of faith. It is by faith the merits of Christ are applied to my soul. But if I am not sincere, they are not applied.

Q. 15. Is not this that *going about to establish your own righteousness,* whereof *St. Paul* speaks, *Rom.* x. 4.

A. *St. Paul* there manifestly speaks of unbelievers, who sought to be accepted for the sake of their own righteousness. We do not seek to be accepted for the sake of our sincerity; but through the merits of Christ alone. Indeed, so long as any man believes, he cannot go about (in *St. Paul's* sense) to *establish his own righteousness.*

Q. 16. But do you consider, that we are under the covenant of grace? [Page 44] And that the covenant of works is now abolished?

A. All mankind were under the covenant of grace, from the very hour that the original promise was made. If by the covenant of works you mean, that of unsinning obedience made with *Adam* before the fall: no man, but *Adam,* was ever under that covenant: for it was abolished before *Cain* was born. Yet it is not so abolished, but that it will stand, in a measure, even to the end of the world, *i.e.* if we *do this,* we shall live; if not, we shall die eternally: if we do well, we shall live with God in glory: if evil, we shall die the second death. For every man shall be judged in that day, and rewarded *according to his works.*

Q. 17. What means then, *to him that believeth, his faith is counted for righteousness?*

A. That God forgives him that is unrighteous as soon as he believes, accepting his faith instead of perfect righteousness. But then observe, universal righteousness follows, though it did not precede faith

[Page 45] Q. 18. But is faith thus *counted to us for righteousness,* at whatsoever time we believe?

A. Yes. In whatsoever moment we believe, all our past sins vanish away. They are as though they had never been, and we stand clear in the sight of God.

Q. 19. Are not the assurance of faith, the inspiration of the Holy Ghost, and the revelation of *Christ* in us, terms nearly of the same import?

A. He that denies one of them, must deny all; they are so closely connected together.

Q. 20. Are they ordinarily, where the pure gospel is preached, essential to our acceptance?

A. Undoubtedly they are; and as such, to be insisted on, in the strongest terms.

Q. 21. Is not the whole dispute of salvation by faith, or by works, a mere *strife of words?*

A. In asserting salvation by faith, we mean this; 1st. That pardon (salvation begun) is received by faith, producing works. 2d. That holiness (salvation continued) is faith working [Page 46] by love. 3d. That heaven (salvation finished) is the reward of this faith.

If you who assert salvation by works, or by faith and works, mean the same thing (understanding by faith, the revelation of Christ in us, by salvation, pardon, holiness, glory) we will not strive with you at all. If you do not, this is not a *strife of words;* but the very vitals, the essence of Christianity is the thing in question.

Q. 22. Wherein does our doctrine now differ from that we preached when at Oxford?

A. Chiefly in these two points: 1st. We then knew nothing of that righteousness of faith, in justification; nor 2d. Of the nature of faith itself, as implying consciousness of pardon.

Q. 23. May not some degree of the love of God, go before a distinct sense of justification?

A. We believe it may.

Q. 24. Can any degree of sanctification or holiness?

A. Many degrees of outward holiness may: yea, and some degree of meekness, and several other tempers which would be branches of Christian [Page 47] holiness, but that they do not spring from Christian principles. For the abiding love of God cannot spring, but from faith in a pardoning God. And no true Christian holiness can exist, without that love of God for its foundation.

Q. 25. Is every man, as soon as he believes, a new creature, sanctified, pure in heart? Has he then a new heart? Does Christ dwell therein? and is he a temple of the Holy Ghost?

A. All these things may be affirmed of every believer, in a true sense. Let us not therefore contradict those who maintain it. Why should we contend about words?

IV. Q. 1. How much is allowed by our brethren who differ from us, with regard to entire sanctification?

A. They grant, 1st. That every one must be entirely sanctified, in the article of death:

2d. That till then a believer daily grows in grace, comes nearer and nearer to perfection:

3d. That we ought to be continually pressing after this, and to exhort all others so to do.

[Page 48]*Q.* 2. What do we allow them?

A. We grant, 1st. That many of those who have died in the faith, yea, the greater part of those we have known, were not sanctified throughout, not made perfect in love, till a little before death:

2d. That the term, 'sanctified' is continually applied by *St. Paul,* to all that were justified, were true believers:

3d. That by this term alone, he rarely (if ever) means, saved from all sin:

4th. That consequently, it is not proper to use it in this sense, without adding the words 'wholly, entirely,' or the like:

5th. That the inspired writers almost continually speak of, or to those who were justified; but very rarely, either of, or to those, who were wholly sanctified:

6th. That consequently, it behoves us to speak in public almost continually of the state of justification: but more rarely, at least in full and explicit terms, concerning entire sanctification.

[Page 49]*Q.* 3. What then is the point where-in we divide?

A. It is this: Whether we should expect to be saved from all sin, before the article of death?

Q. 4. Is there any clear scripture *promise* of this? That God will save us from *all* sin?

A. There is. *Psalm* CXXX. 8. *He shall redeem Israel from* all *his sins.*

This is more largely expressed in the prophecy of *Ezekiel: Then will I sprinkle clean water upon you, and you shall be clean; from* all *your filthiness, and from* all *your idols will I cleanse you—I will also save you from* all *your uncleannesses,* c. xxxvi. v. 25, 29. No promise can be more clear. And to this the apostle plainly refers in that exhortation, *Having these promises, let us cleanse ourselves, from all filthiness of flesh and spirit, perfecting holiness in the fear of God.* 2 *Cor.* vii. 1. Equally clear and express is that ancient promise, *The Lord thy God will circumcise thine heart and the heart of thy seed, to love the Lord thy God with all thy heart and with all thy soul.* Deut. xxx. 6.

[Page 50]Q. 5. But does any *assertion* answerable to this, occur in the New Testament?

A. There does, and that laid down in the plainest terms. So *St. John* iii. 8. *For this purpose the Son of God was manifested, that he might destroy the works of the Devil.* The works of the Devil, without any limitation or restriction: but all sin is the work of the Devil. Parallel to which is that assertion of *St. Paul, Eph.* v. 25, 27. *Christ loved the church and gave himself for it—that he might present it to himself a glorious church, not having spot or wrinkle or any such thing, but that it should be holy and without blemish.*

And to the same effect is that assertion in the viiith of the *Romans* (v. S, 4.) *God sent his Son—that the righteousness of the law might be fulfilled in us, walking not after the flesh but after the Spirit.*

Q. 6. Does the New Testament afford any further ground, for expecting to be saved from all sin?

A. Undoubtedly it does, both in those prayers and commands which [Page 51] are equivalent to the strongest assertions.

Q. 7. What prayers do you mean?

A. Prayers for entire sanctification; which, were there no such thing, would be mere mockery of God. Such in particular, are 1. *Deliver us from evil;* or rather, *from the evil one.* Now when this is done, when we are delivered from all evil, there can be no sin remaining. 2. *Neither pray I for these alone, but for them also which shall believe on me through their word: that they all may be one, as thou Father art in me and I in Thee, that they also may be one in us: I in them and thou in me, that they may be made perfect in one. John* xvii. 20, 21, 23.

3. *I bow my knees unto the God and Father of our Lord* Jesus Christ—*that he would grant you—that ye being rooted and grounded in love, may be able to comprehend with all saints, what is the breadth and length and height; and to know the love of* Christ *which passeth knowledge, that ye might be filled with all the fulness of God. Eph.* iii. 14, 16, 19.—4. *The very God of Peace sanctify you wholly. And I pray*[Page 52]*God, your whole spirit, soul, and body, be preserved blameless unto the coming of our Lord* Jesus Christ. 1 *Thess.* v. 23.

Q. 8. What command is there to the same effect?

A. *Be ye perfect as your Father which is in heaven is perfect. Matt.* vi. ult.

2. *Thou shalt love the Lord thy God with all thy heart, and with all thy soul, and with all thy mind. Matt.* xxii. 37. But if the love of God fill all the heart, there can be no sin there.

Q. 9. But how does it appear, that this is to be done before the article of death?

A. First, from the very nature of a command, which is not given to the dead, but to the living.

Therefore, *Thou shalt love the Lord thy God with all thy heart,* cannot mean, Thou shalt do this when thou diest, but while thou livest.

Secondly, from express texts of scripture:

1. *The grace of God that bringeth salvation hath appeared to all men;* [Page 53] *teaching us, that having renounced ungodliness and worldly lusts, we should live soberly, righteously, and godly in this present world: looking for—the glorious appearing of our Lord* Jesus Christ; *who gave himself for us, that he might redeem us from* all *iniquity; and purify unto himself a peculiar people, zealous of good works. Tit.* ii. 11—14.

2. *He hath raised up an horn of salvation for us—to perform the mercy promised to our fathers; the oath which he swore to our father* Abraham, *that he would grant unto us, that we being delivered out of the hands of our enemies, should serve him without fear, in holiness and righteousness before him all the days of our life. Luke* i. 69, &c.

Q. 10. Does not the harshly preaching perfection tend to bring believers into a kind of bondage, or slavish fear?

A. It does. Therefore we should always place it in the most amiable light, so that it may excite only hope, joy, and desire.

Q. 11. Why may we not continue in the joy of faith even till we are made perfect?

[Page 54]*A.* Why, indeed? Since holy grief does not quench this joy: since even while we are under the cross, while we deeply partake of the sufferings of Christ, we may rejoice with joy unspeakable.

Q. 12. Do we not discourage believers from rejoicing evermore?

A. We ought not so to do. Let them all their life long rejoice unto God, so it be with reverence. And even if lightness or pride should mix with their joy, let us not strike at the joy itself (this is the gift of God) but at that lightness or pride, that the evil may cease and the good remain.

Q. 13. Ougnt we to be anxiously careful about perfection? Lest we should die before we have attained?

A. In no wise. We ought to be thus *careful for nothing,* neither spiritual nor temporal.

Q. 14. But ought we not to be *troubled,* on account of the sinful nature which still remains in us?

A. It is good for us to have a deep sense of this, and to be much ashamed before the Lord. But this should only incite us, the more earnestly to turn [Page 55] unto Christ every moment, and to draw light and life, and strength from him, that we may go on, conquering and to conquer. And therefore, when the sense of our sin most abounds, the sense of his love should much more abound.

Q. 15. Will our joy or our trouble increase as we grow in grace?

A. Perhaps both. But without doubt our joy in the Lord will increase as our love increases.

Q. 16. Is not the teaching believers to be continually poring over their inbred sin, the ready way to make them forget that they were purged from their former sins?

A. We find by experience, it is; or to make them under-value, and account it a little thing: whereas indeed (though there are still greater gifts behind) this is inexpressibly great and glorious.

SECTION III.

Of the General Conference or Convention.

Quest. 1. Who shall compose the General Conference or Convention, [Page 56] and what are the regulations and powers belonging to it?

Answ. 1. The General Conference or Convention shall be composed of one delegate for every two hundred members belonging to our society, who shall be nominated by the Quarterly Meeting Conference, and appointed by the male members of society, according to the charters or constitutions of the different African Churches belonging to our society; but no minister or preacher shall be eligible to the office of delegate, until he has been licensed according to our discipline, for at least two years.

2. The General Conference or Convention shall meet on the first Monday in May, once in every four years, at such place as shall be fixed on by the General Conference or Convention, from time to time. But the General Superintendant, with the consent of any two ministers having the charge, and the concurrence of two-thirds of any two Quarterly Conferences, may call a General Conference or Convention.

3. At all times when the General [Page 57] Conference or Convention is met, it shall take two-thirds of the members to transact business.

4. The General Superintendant's duty shall be, to preside in all our Conferences or Conventions. But in case no General Superintendant be present, the Assistant shall act in his place: but, in their absence, the Conference shall choose a President pro tempore.

5. The General Conference or Convention shall have all power to make rules and regulations for our church, under the following limitations and restrictions, viz.

1. The General Conference or Convention shall not revoke, alter, or change our articles of religion, nor establish any new standards or rules of doctrine contrary to our present existing and established standards of doctrine.

2. They shall not change or alter any part or rule of our government, so as to do away Episcopacy, or destroy the plan of our itinerant general superintendancy.[Page 58]

3. They shall not do away the privileges of our ministers or preachers of trial by a committee, and of an appeal: Neither shall they do away the privileges of our members of trial before the society or by a committee, and of an appeal.

Of the Yearly Conferences.

Quest. 1. Who shall attend the Yearly Conferences?

Answ. All the preachers who have been licensed two years, at the time of holding the Conference. But the Conference shall act according to their judgment as to the standing of a preacher, previous to his obtaining license from the preacher having the charge, (in behalf of the Quarterly Conference;) and the Annual Conference may admit him a full member if they think proper.

Q. 2. Who shall appoint the times of holding the Yearly Conferences?

A. The General Superintendant; but he shall allow the Conference to sit a week at least.

Q. 3. Who shall appoint the places of holding the Annual Conferences?

[Page 59]A. Each Annual Conference shall appoint the place of its own sitting.

Q. 4. What is the method wherein we usually proceed in the Yearly Conferences?

A. We inquires,

1. What preachers are admitted on trial? 2. Who remain on trial? 3. Who are admitted into full connection? 4. Who are the deacons? 5. Who have been elected and ordained elders this year? 6. Who have been elected by the General Conference or Convention, to exercise the Episcopal Office, and superintend the African Methodist Church in America? 7. Who have located this year? 8. Who are the supernumeraries?* 9. Who have been expelled from the connection this year?[Page 60] 10. Who have withdrawn from the connection this year? 11. Are all the preachers blameless in life and conversation? 12. Who have died this year? 13. What numbers are in society? 14. What has been collected for th contingent expenses, for the making up the allowances of the preachers, &c.? 15. How has this been expended? 16. Where are the preachers stationed this year? 17. Where and when shall our next Conference be held?

Q. 18. Is there any other business to be done in the Yearly Conferences?

A. The electing and ordaining of elders and deacons.

Q. 19. Are there any other directions to be given, concerning the Yearly Conferences?

A. There shall be at least two Conferences in the year: One in Baltimore and one in Philadelphia. The first shall be in Baltimore.

A record of the proceedings of each Annual Conference shall be kept by [Page 61] a secretary, chosen for that purpose, and shall be signed by the president and secretary: and let a copy of the said record, be sent to the General Conference or Convention.

SECTION IV.

Of the Election and Consecration of a General Superintendant, and of his duty.

Quest. 1. How is a General Superintendant to be constituted?

---

* A supernumerary preacher is one so worn out in the itinerant service, as to be rendered incapable of preaching constantly; but at the same time, is willing to do any work in the ministry, which the conference may direct, and his strength enable him to perform.

Answ. By the election of the General Conference or Convention, and the laying on of the hands of a General Superintendant and two elders; or for want of elders, two deacons or preachers.

Q. 2. If by death, expulsion, or otherwise, there be no General Superintendant in our Church, what shall we do?

A. The General Superintendant's Assistant shall call a General Conference or Convention to appoint one; and in the interval the Assistant shall discharge his duties.

Q. 3. What shall be done, if by death, expulsion, or otherwise, there [Page 62] be no Assistant to the General Superintendant?

A. The General Superintendant shall choose one, to act until the sitting of the next General Conference or Convention. And should it so happen, that we have no General Superintendant or Assistant, then two elders shall call a General Conference or Convention, to fill the vacancies.

Q. 4. What are the duties of the General Superintendant?

A. 1. To preside in all our Conferences.

2. To fix all the appointments of the travelling ministers, in conjunction with his Assistant, at the Annual Conferences; (but in the interval of the conference, he shall exercise his judgment, in conjunction with the preacher having the charge, and the Quarterly Conference where he wishes the preacher removed from.

3. To travel through the connection at large.

4. To oversee the spiritual business of the societies.

5. To ordain General Superintendants, Elders, and Deacons.

[Page 63] Q. 5. To whom is a General Superintendant amenable for his conduct?

A. To the General Conference or Convention, who have power to expel him for improper conduct, if they think proper.

Q. 6. What provision shall be made for the trial of a General Superintendant, in the interval of a General Conference or Convention?

A. He shall be examined by three Elders, or two Elders and a Deacon: they shall have power to suspend him from the superintendancy, and shall give him a copy of the charge. And the Assistant shall call together the members of an Annual Conference; and the said Annual Conference shall have power to suspend him from all official standing, until the ensuing General Conference or Convention, where it shall be finally determined: but all accusations shall be given to him at his first trial, by those who are to prove the crime.

Q. 7. If a General Superintendant cease from travelling at large among the people, shall he still exercise the episcopal office among us in any degree?

[Page 64]A. This shall be regulated by the General Conference or Convention; and they shall make provision for defraying his travelling expenses.

SECTION V.

Of bringing to Trial, finding Guilty, and reproving, suspending, or excluding, disorderly Persons from Society and Church Privileges.

Quest. How shall an accused member be brought to trial?

Answ. 1. Before the society of which he is a member, or a select number of them, in the presence of a General Superintendant, Elder, Deacon, or Preacher, in the following manner: Let the accused and accuser be brought face to face; but if this cannot be done, let the next best evidence be procured. If the accused person be found guilty by the decision of a majority of the members before whom he is brought to trial, and the crime be such as is expressly forbidden by the word of God, sufficient to exclude a person from the kingdom of grace and glory, let the Minister or Preacher [Page 65] who has the charge of the circuit, expel him. If the accused person evade a trial, by absenting himself, after sufficient notice given him, and the circumstances of the accusation be strong and presumptive, let him be esteemed as guilty, and be accordingly excluded. Witnesses from without, shall not be rejected.

2. But in cases of neglect of duties of any kind, imprudent conduct, indulging sinful tempers or words, or disobedience to the order and discipline of the church:—First, let private reproof be given by a preacher or leader; and if there be an acknowledgment of the truth, and proper humiliation, the person may remain on trial. On a second offence, the preacher or leader may take one or two faithful friends. On a third offence, let the case be brought before the society, or a select number; and if there be no sign of real humiliation, the offender must be cut off.

3. If a member of our church shall be clearly convicted of endeavouring to sow dissentions in any of our societies, by inveighing against either [Page 66] our doctrines or discipline, such person so offending, shall be

first reproved by the senior minister or preacher of his circuit; and, if he afterwards persist in such pernicious practices, he shall be expelled the society.

4. On any dispute between two or more members of our society, concerning the payment of debts or otherwise, which cannot be settled by the parties concerned, the preacher who has the charge of the circuit or station, shall inquire into the circumstances of the case; and shall recommend to the contending parties a reference, consisting of one arbiter chosen by the plaintiff, and another chosen by the defendant; which two arbiters, so chosen, shall nominate a third: the three arbiters being members of our society.

5. But if one of the parties be dissatisfied with the judgment given, such party may apply to the ensuing Quarterly Meeting of the circuit or station, for permission to have a second arbitration appointed; and if the Quarterly Meeting see sufficient reason, they shall grant a second arbitration: [Page 67] In which case, each party shall choose two arbiters, and the four arbiters shall choose a fifth, the judgement of the majority of whom shall be final; and any person refusing to abide by such judgment, shall be excluded the society.

6. And if any member of our society shall refuse, in cases of debt, or other disputes, to refer the matter to arbitration, when recommended by him who has the charge of the circuit, or shall enter into a law suit with another member before these measures are taken, he shall be expelled, excepting the case be of such a nature as to require and justify a process at law.

7. The preachers who have the oversight of circuits are required to execute all our rules fully and strenuously against all fraud, and particularly against dishonest insolvencies: suffering none to remain in our society, on any account, who are found guilty of any fraud.

8. To prevent scandal, when any of our members fail in business, or contract debts which they are not [Page 68] able to pay, let two or three judicious members of the society inspect the accounts of the supposed delinquent; and if he have behaved dishonestly, or borrowed money without a probability of paying, let him be expelled.

9. Whenever a complaint is made against any member of our church, for non payment of debt; when the accounts are adjusted and the amount ascertained, the preacher having the charge shall call the debtor before a committee of at least three, to shew cause why he does not make payment. The committee shall determine what further time shall be granted him

for payment, and what security if any, shall be given for payment; and in case the debtor refuses to comply, he shall be expelled: but in such case he may appeal to the Quarterly Meeting Conference and their decision shall be final. And in case the creditor complains that justice is not done him, he may lay his grievance before the Quarterly Meeting Conference, and their decision shall be final; and if the creditor refuses to comply, he shall be expelled.

[Page 69]10. Nevertheless, if in any of the abovememtioned cases, the minister or preacher differ in judgment from the majority of the society, or the select number, concerning the innocence or guilt of the accused person, the trial in such case may be referred by the minister or preacher, to the ensuing Quarterly Meeting.

11. If there be a murmur or complaint from any excluded person in any of the abovementioned instances, that justice has not been done, he shall be allowed to appeal to the next Quarterly Meeting, except such as absent themselves from trial, after sufficient notice is given them, and the majority of the travelling and local preachers, exhorters, stewards, and leaders present, shall finally determine the case.

After such forms of trial and expulsion, such person shall have no privileges of society or of sacrament in our church, without contrition, confession and proper trial.

[Page 70] *SECTION VI.*

Of the Duty of Elders having the Charge.

Quest. 1. How is an elder constituted?

Answ. By the election of a majority of the Yearly Conference, and by the laying on of the hands of a General Superintendant, and some of the Elders present.

Q. 2. What are the duties of an Elder having the charge?

A. 1. In the absence of the General Superintendant, to take charge of all the elders and deacons, travelling and local preachers and exhorters, in his charge.

2. To be present at all the Quarterly Meetings; to preside in the Quarterly Conferences, (consisting of all the travelling and local preachers, exhorters, stewards, and class leaders, belonging to his charge, and none else;)

to hear complaints, and try appeals. The Quarterly Conference shall appoint a secretary, to take down the proceedings of each Quarterly [Page 71] Conference, in a book kept by one of the stewards of his charge for that purpose.

3. To take care that every part of our discipline be enforced in his charge.

4. To attend the General Superintendant when present in his charge, and to give him when absent, all necessary information by letter, of the state of his charge.

Q. 2. Shall he have power to employ a preacher who has been rejected at the previous Annual Conference?

A. 1. He shall not, without the consent of a majority of the Quarterly Conference, and permission from the said Annual Conference so to do.

2. He shall travel, and labour through his charge; administer Baptism and the Lord's Supper, perform the office of Matrimony, and all parts of Divine worship.

3. He shall not cease to travel without the consent of the Yearly Conference, certified under the hand of the President of the Conference; except in case of sickness, debility, [Page 72] or other unavoidable circumstances. Nevertheless, the final determination of all such cases, is with the Annual Conference.

4. To meet the societies, classes, and general bands.

5. To visit the sick.

6. To be diligent: never be unemployed; never be triflingly employed.

7. To see that the other preachers in his circuit behave well, and want nothing.

8. To renew the tickets quarterly, and regulate the bands.

9. To meet the stewards and leaders as often as possible.

10. To appoint all the leaders, and change them when he sees it necessary: (but the stewards shall be appointed in the way the discipline directs.)

11. To receive, try, and expel members, according to the form of discipline.

12. To hold watch nights and love feats.

13. To hold Quarterly Meetings.

14. To take care that every society be duly supplied with books.

[Page 73]15. To take an exact account of the numbers in society, in their respective circuits or stations, and deliver in such account to the Annual Conference, that they may be printed in the minutes.

16. To meet the men and women apart in the large societies, once a quarter, wherever it is practicable.

17. To overlook the accounts of all the stewards.

18. To appoint a person to receive the quarterly collection in the classes, (where there is no steward.)

19. To see that public collections be made quarterly, if need be.

20. To raise a yearly subscription in those circuits that can bear it, for building Churches, and paying the debts of those which have been already erected.

21. To choose a committee of laymembers, to make a just application of the money where it is most wanted, (where there is no steward.)

Q. 3. What other directions shall we give him?

A. Several:

1. To leave his successor a particular [Page 74] account of the state of the circuit.

2. To see that every Band-leader have the rules of the bands.

3. To enforce vigorously, but calmly, all the rules of the society.

4. As soon as there are four men or women believers in any place, to put them into a band.

5. He may suffer the love feast to last an hour and a half.

6. To warn all from time to time, that none are to remove from one circuit to another, without a note of recommendation from a preacher of the circuit, in these words: *"A. B. the bearer, has been an acceptable member of our Society in C."* and to inform them, that without such a certificate, they will not be received into other societies.

7. To recommend every where decency and cleanliness.

8. To read the rules of the society with the aid of the other preachers, once a year in every congregation, and once a quarter in every society.

9. He shall take care that a fast be held in every society in his circuit, on [Page 75] the Friday preceding every Quarterly Meeting; and that a memorandum of it be written on all the class-papers.

10. He shall also take care, that no unordained local preacher or exhorter in his circuit, shall officiate in public, without first obtaining a license from the Elder having the charge. Let every unordained local preacher and exhorter take care to have this renewed yearly; and let him who has the charge of the circuit insist upon it.

SECTION VII.

Of the Trial of those who think they are moved by the Holy Ghost to preach.

Quest. How shall we try those who profess to be moved by the Holy Ghost to preach?

Answ. 1. Let them be asked the following questions, viz. Do they know God as a pardoning God? Have they the love of God abiding in them? Do they desire and seek nothing but God? Are they holy in all manner of conversation?

2. Have they gifts (as well as grace) [Page 76] for the work? Have they (in some tolerable degree) a clear, sound understanding, a right judgment in the things of God, a just conception of salvation by faith? And has God given them any degree of utterance? Do they speak justly, readily, clearly?

3. Have they fruit? Are any truly convinced of sin, and converted to God by their preaching?

As long as these three marks concur in any one, we believe he is called of God to preach. These we receive as sufficient proof that he is moved by the Holy Ghost.

SECTION VIII.

Of the Matter and Manner of Preaching, and other public Exercises.

Quest. 1. What is the best general method of preaching?

Answ. 1. To convince: 2. To offer Christ: 3. To invite: 4. To build up: And to do this in some measure, in every sermon.

Q. 2. What is the most effectual way of preaching Christ?

A. The most effectual way of preaching [Page 77] Christ, is to preach him in all his offices; and to declare his law, as well as his gospel, both to believers and unbelievers. Let us strongly and closely insist upon inward and outward holiness in all its branches.

Q. 3. Are there any smaller advices which might be of use to us?

A. Perhaps these: 1. Be sure never to disappoint a congregation. 2. Begin at the time appointed. 3. Let your whole deportment be serious, weighty, and solemn. 4. Always suit your subject to your audience. 5. Choose the plainest text you can. 6. Take care not to ramble, but keep to your text, and make out what you take in hand. 7. Take care of any thing aukward or affected, either in your gesture, phrase, or pronunciation. 8. Do not usually pray ex tempore above eight or ten minutes (at most) without intermission. 9. Frequently read and enlarge upon a portion of scripture; and let young preachers often exhort without taking a text. 10. Always avail yourself of the great festivals, by preaching on the occasion.

[Page 78] *SECTION IX.*

Of the Duty of Preachers to God, themselves, and one another.

Quest. 1. How shall a preacher be qualified for his charge?

Answ. By walking closely with God and having his work greatly at heart: And by understanding and loving discipline, ours in particular.

Q. 2. Do we sufficiently watch over each other?

A. We do not. Should we not frequently ask each other, Do you walk closely with God? Have you now fellowship with the Father and the Son? At what hour do you rise? Do you punctually observe the morning and evening hour of retirement? Do you spend the day in the manner which the Conference advises? Do you converse seriously, usefully, and closely? To be more particular: Do you use all the means of grace yourself, and enforce the use of them on all persons? They are instituted or prudential.

The instituted are,

1. Prayer; private, family, public; consisting of deprecation, petition, intercession, [Page 79] and thanksgiving. Do you use each of these? Do you forecast daily wherever you are, to secure time for private devotion? Do you practise it every where? Do you ask every where, Have you family prayer? Do you ask individuals, Do you use private prayer every morning and evening in particular?

2. Searching the scriptures, by

(1) Reading; constantly, some part of every day: regularly, all the Bible in order: carefully, with notes: seriously, with prayer before and after: fruitfully, immediately practising what you learn there?

(2) Meditating: At set times? By rule?

(3) Hearing: Every opportunity? With prayer before, at, after? Have you a Bible always about you?

3. The Lord's Supper: Do you use this at every opportunity? With solemn prayer before? With earnest and deliberate self-devotion?

4. Fasting: Do you use as much abstinence and fasting every week, as your health, strength, and labour will permit?

[Page 80]5. Christian conference: Are you convinced how important and how difficult it is to order your conversation aright? Is it always in grace? Seasoned with salt? Meet to minister grace to the hearers? Do you not converse too long at a time? Is not an hour commonly enough? Would it not be well always to have a determinate end in view? And to pray before and after it?

II. Prudential means we may use, either as Christians, as Methodists, or as Preachers.

1. As Christians: What particular rules have you, in order to grow in grace? What arts of holy living?

2. As Methodists: Do you never miss your class or band?

3. As Preachers: Have you thoroughly considered your duty? And do you make a conscience of executing every part of it? Do you meet every society? Also, the leaders and bands?

These means may be used without fruit. But there are some means which cannot; namely, watching, denying ourselves, taking up our cross, exercise of the presence of God.

[Page 81]1. Do you steadily watch against the world? Yourself? Your besetting sin?

2. Do you deny yourself every useless pleasure of sense? Imagination? Honour? Are you temperate in all things? Instance food. Do you use only that kind, and that degree, which is best both for your body and soul? Do you see the necessity of this? Do you eat no more at each meal than is necessary? Are you not heavy or drowsy after dinner? 3. Do you use only that kind and that degree of drink which is best for your body and soul? 4. Do you choose and use water, for your common drink? And only take wine medicinally or sacramentally?

3. Wherein do you take up your cross daily? Do you cheerfully bear your cross, however grievous to nature, as a gift of God, and labour to profit thereby?

4. Do you endeavour to set God always before you? To see his eye continually fixed upon you? Never can you use these means, but a blessing will ensue. And the more you use them, the more will you grow in grace.

[Page 82] *SECTION X.*

Rules by which we should continue, or desist from, preaching at any place.

Quest. 1. Is it advisable for us to preach in as many places as we can, without forming any societies?

Answ. By no means: We have made the trial in various places; and that for a considerable time. But all the seed has fallen by the way side. There is scarce any fruit remaining.

Q. 2. Where should we endeavour to preach most?

A. 1. Where there are the greatest number of quiet and willing hearers.

2. Where there is the most fruit.

Q. 3. Ought we net diligently to observe, in what places God is pleased at any time to pour out his Spirit more abundantly?

A. We ought: And at that time, to send more labourers than usual into that part of the harvest.

SECTION XI.

Of visiting from house to house; guarding against those sins that are so common to professors, and enforcing practical religion.

[Page 83] *Quest.* 1. How can we further assist those under our care?

Answ. By instructing them at their own houses. What unspeakable need is there of this! The world says, "*The Methodists are no better than other people.*" This is not true in the general. But, 1. Personal religion, either toward God or man, is too superficial amongst us. We can but just touch on a few particulars. How little faith is there among us? How little communion with God? How little living in Heaven, walking in eternity, deadness to every creature? How much love of the world? Desire of pleasure, of ease, of getting money? How little brotherly love? What continual judging one another? What gossipping, evil-speaking, tale-bearing? What want of moral honesty? To instance only one particular; who does as he would be done by, in buying and selling?

2. Family religion is wanting in many branches. And what avails public [Page 84] preaching alone, though we could preach like angels? We

must, yea, every travelling preacher must instruct the people from house to house. Till this is done, and that in good earnest, the Methodists will be no better.

Our religion is not deep, universal, uniform; but superficial, partial, uneven. It will be so till we spend half as much in this visiting, as we do now in talking uselessly. Can we find a better method of doing this than Mr. Baxter's? If not, let us adopt it without delay. His whole tract, entitled, *Gildas Salvianus,* is well worth a careful perusal. Speaking of this visiting from house to house, he says (p. 351.)

"We shall find many hindrances, both in ourselves and the people.

1. In ourselves, there is much dulness and laziness, so that there will be much ado to get us to be faithful in the work.

2. We have a base, man-pleasing temper, so that we let men perish, rather than lose their love: we let them go quietly to hell, let we should offend them.

[Page 85]3. Some of us have also a foolish bashfulness. We know not how to begin; and blush to contradict the devil.

4. But the greatest hindrance is weakness of faith. Our whole motion is weak, because the spring of it is weak.

5. Lastly, we are unskilful in the work. How few know how to deal with men, so as to get within them, and suit all our discourse to their several conditions and tempers: To choose the fittest subjects, and follow them with a holy mixture of seriousness, terror, love, and meekness?"

But undoubtedly this private application is implied in those solemn words of the apostle, *I charge thee before God and the Lord Jesus Christ, who shall judge the quick and dead at his appearing, preach the word; be instant in season, out of season: Reprove, rebuke, exhort, with all long suffering.*

O brethren, if we could but set this work on foot in all our societies, and prosecute it zealously, what glory would redound to God! If the common lukewarmness were banished, [Page 86] and every shop and every house busied in speaking of the word and works of God; surely God would dwell in our habitations, and make us his delight.

And this is absolutely necessary to the welfare of our people, some of whom neither repent nor believe to this day. Look round, and see how many of them are still in apparent danger of damnation. And how can you walk, and talk, and be merry with such people, when you know their case? Methinks when you look them in the face, you should break forth into tears, as the prophet did when he looked upon Hazael, and then set on them with the most vehement exhortations. O, for God's sake, and the sake of poor souls, bestir yourselves, and spare no pains that may conduce to their salvation!

What cause have we to bleed before the Lord, that we have so long neglected this good work! If we had but engaged in it sooner, how many more might have been brought to Christ? And how much holier and happier might we have made our societies [Page 87] before now? And why might we not have done it sooner? There were many hindrances: And so there always will be. But the greatest hindrance was in ourselves, in our littleness of faith and love.

But it is objected, I. "This will take up so much time, we shall not have leisure to follow our studies."

We answer, 1. Gaining knowledge is a good thing, but saving souls is better. 2. By this very thing you will gain the most excellent knowledge, that of God and eternity. 3. You will have time for gaining other knowledge too. Only sleep not more than you need: "and never be idle or triflingly employed." But 4. If you can do but one, let your studies alone. We ought to throw by all the libraries in the world, rather than be guilty of the loss of one soul.

It is objected, II. "The people will not submit to it." If some will not, others will. And the success with them, will repay all your labour. O let us herein follow the example of St. Paul. 1. For our general business, *Serving the Lord with all humility of*[Page 88]*mind:* 2. Our special work, *Take heed to yourselves, and to all the flock:* 3. Our doctrine, *Repentance towards God, and faith towards our Lord Jesus Christ:* 4. The place, *I have taught you publicly, and from house to house:* 5. The object and manner of teaching, *I ceased not to warn every one, night and day, with tears:* 6. His innocence and self-denial herein, *I have coveted no man's silver or gold:* 7. His patience, *Neither count I my life dear unto myself.* And among all other motives, let these be ever before our eyes: 1. *The church of God, which he hath purchased with his own blood.* 2. Grievous wolves shall enter in: yea, of yourselves, shall men arise, speaking perverse things.

Write this upon your hearts, and it will do you more good than twenty years' study. Then you will have no time to spare: You will have work enough. Then likewise no preacher will stay with us who is as salt that has lost its savour. For to such this employment would be mere drudgery. And in order to it, you will have need of all the knowledge you can procure, and grace you can attain.

[Page 89]The sum is, Go into every house in course, and teach every one therein, young and old, to be Christians inwardly and outwardly; make every particular plain to their understandings; fix it in their minds; write it on their hearts. In order to this, there must be line upon line, precept upon precept. What patience, what love, what knowledge is requisite for this! We must needs do this, were it only to avoid idleness. Do we not loiter away many hours in every week? Each try himself: No idleness is consistent with growth in grace. Nay, without exactness in redeeming time, you cannot retain the grace you received in justification.

Q. 2. Why are we not more holy, why do we not live in eternity? Walk with God all the day long? Why are we not all devoted to God? Breathing the whole spirit of missionaries?

A. Chiefly because we are enthusiasts, looking for the end without using the means. To touch only upon two or three instances: Who of us rises at four? Or even at five, when we do not preach? Do we know the [Page 90] obligation and benefit of fasting or abstinence? How often do we practise it? The neglect of this alone is sufficient to account for our feebleness and faintness of spirit. We are continually grieving the Holy Spirit of God by the habitual neglect of a plain duty. Let us amend from this hour.

Q. 3. How shall we guard against sabbath-breaking, evil-speaking, unprofitable conversation, lightness, expensiveness or gaiety of apparel, and contracting debts without due care to discharge them?

A. Let us preach expressly on each of these heads.

SECTION XII.

Of the Instruction of Children.

Quest. What shall we do for the rising generation?

Answ. 1. Let him who is zealous for God and the souls of men begin now.

2. Where there are ten children whose parents are in society, meet them an hour once a week; but where this is impracticable, meet them once in two weeks.

[Page 91]3. Procure our instructions or Catechisms for them, and let all who can, read and commit them to memory.

4. Explain and impress them upon their hearts.

5. Talk with them every time you see any at home.

6. Pray earnestly for them: And diligently instruct and exhort all parents at their own houses.

7. Let the Elders, Deacons, and Preachers, take a list of the names of the children; and if any of them be truly awakened, let them be admitted into society.

8. Preach expressly on education: "But I have no gift for this." Pray earnestly for the gift, and use every other means to attain it.

SECTION XIII.

Of Baptism.

1. LET every adult person and the parents of every child to be baptised, have the choice either of immersion, sprinkling, or pouring.

2. We will on no account whatever receive a present for administering baptism, or for burying the dead.

[Page 92] SECTION XIV.

Of the Lord's Supper.

Quest. ARE there any directions to be given concerning the administration of the Lord's Supper?

Answ. 1. Let those who have scruples concerning the receiving of it kneeling, be permitted to receive it either standing or sitting.

2. Let no person that is not a member of our society, be admitted to the communion, without examination, and some token given by an elder or deacon.

3. No person shall be admitted to the Lord's Supper among us, who is guilty of any practice for which we would exclude a member of our church.

SECTION XV.

Of Public Worship.

Quest. WHAT directions shall be given for the establishment of uniformity in pubilc worship amongst us, on the Lord's day?

[Page 93]*Answ.* 1. Let the morning service consist of singing, prayer, the reading of a chapter out of the Old Testament, and another out of the New, and preaching.

2. Let the afternoon service consist of singing, prayer, the reading of one or two chapters out of the Bible, and preaching.

3. Let the evening service consist of singing, prayer, and preaching.

4. But on the days of administering the Lord's Supper, the two chapters in the morning service may be omitted

5. Let the society be met, wherever it is practicable, on the sabbath-day.

SECTION XVI.

Of the Spirit and Truth of Singing.

Quest. How shall we guard against formality in singing?

Answ. 1. By choosing such hymns as are proper for the congregation.

2. By not singing too much at once; seldom more than five or six verses.

[Page 94]3. By suiting the tune to the words.

4. By often stopping short, and asking the people, "Now! do you know what you said last? Did you speak no more than you felt?"

5. Do not suffer the people to sing too slow. This naturally tends to formality; and is brought in by those who have either very strong or very weak voices.

6. In every large society let them learn to sing; and let them always learn our tunes first.

7. Let the women constantly sing their parts alone. Let no man sing with them unless he understands the notes, and sings the bass as it is composed in the tune book.

8. Introduce no new tune till they are perfect in the old.

9. Recommend our Tune-book.—And if you cannot sing yourself, choose a person or two at each place to pitch the tune for you.

10. Exhort every person in the congregation to sing; not one in ten only.

11. Sing no hymns of your own composing.

[Page 95]12. If a preacher be present, let him alone give out the words.

13. When the singers would teach a tune to the congregation, they must sing only the tenor.

14. Let it be recommended to our people, not to attend the singing-schools which are not under our direction.

15. The preachers are desired not to encourage the singing of fuge-tunes in our congregations.

16. We do not think that fuge-tunes are sinful, or improper to be used in private companies: but we do not approve of their being used in our public congregations, because public singing is a part of divine worship, in which all the congregation ought to join.

[Page 96] CHAPTER II.

SECTION I.

The Nature, Design, and general Rules of the United Societies.

(1) IN the latter end of the year 1739, eight or ten persons came to Mr. Wesley in London, who appeared to be deeply convinced of sin, and earnestly groaning for redemption. They desired (as did two or three more the next day) that he would spend some time with them in prayer, and advise them how to flee from the wrath to come; which they saw continually hanging over their heads. That he might have more time for this great work, he appointed a day when they might all come together, which from thence forward they did every week, namely on *Thursday* in the evening. To these, and as many more as desired to join with them (for their number increased daily) he gave those advices from time to time which he judged most needful for them; and they always concluded their meeting with prayer, suited to their several necessities.

[Page 97] (2) This was the rise of the UNITED SOCIETY, first in *Europe*, and then in *America*. Such a society is no other than "*a company of men having the form and seeking the power of Godliness, united in order to pray together, to receive the word of exhortation, and to watch over one another in love, that they may help each other to work out their salvation.*"

(3) That it may the more easily be discerned, whether they are indeed working out their own salvation, each society is divided into smaller companies, (called classes) according to their respective places of abode.—There

are about twelve persons in a class; one of whom is stiled *"The Leader."* It is his duty,

I. To see each person in his class once a week at least; in order

1. To inquire how their souls prosper:

2. To advise, reprove, comfort, or exhort, as occasion may require:

3. To receive what they are willing to give, towards the relief of the preachers, church, and poor.

[Page 98]II. To meet the ministers and the stewards of the society once a week; in order

1. To inform the minister of any that are sick, or of any that walk disorderly, and will not be reproved.

2. To pay the stewards what they have received of their several classes in the week preceding.

(4) There is only one condition previously required of those who desire admission into these societies, *a desire to flee from the wrath to come, and to be saved from their sins.* But wherever this is really fixed in the soul, it will be shewn by its fruits.—It is therefore expected of all who continue therein, that they should continue to evidence their desire of salvation,

First, By doing no harm, by avoiding evil of every kind, especially that which is most generally practised: such as,

The taking the name of God in vain.

The profaning the day of the Lord, either by doing ordinary work therein, or by buying and selling.

[Page 99]Drunkenness: or drinking spirituous liquors, unless in cases of necessity.

The buying and selling of men, women, and children, with an intention to enslave them.

Fighting, quarrelling, brawling, brother *going to law* with brother; returning evil for evil; or railing for railing; the *using many words* in buying and selling.

The buying or selling goods that have not paid the duty.

The giving or taking things on usury, i. e. unlawful interest.

Uncharitable or unprofitable conversation: particularly speaking evil of magistrates or of ministers.

Doing to others as we would not they should do unto us.

Doing what we know is not for the glory of God: As

The putting on of gold and costly apparel.

The taking such diversions as cannot be used in the name of the Lord Jesus.

The *singing* those *songs*, or *reading*[Page 100] those *books*, which do not tend to the knowledge or love of God.

Softness, and needless self-indulgence.

Laying up treasure upon earth.

Borrowing without a probability of paying; or taking up goods without a probability of paying for them.

(5) It is expected of all who continue in these societies, that they should continue to evidence their desire of salvation,

Secondly, By doing good, by being in every kind, merciful according to their power; as they have opportunity, doing good of every possible sort, and as far as is possible, to all men:

To their bodies of the ability which God giveth, by giving food to the hungry, by clothing the naked, by visiting or helping them that are sick, or in prison.

To their souls, by instructing, reproving or exhorting all we have any intercourse with; trampling under foot that enthusiastic doctrine, that "we are not to do good, unless *our hearts be free to it.*"

By doing good, especially to them [Page 101] that are of the household of faith, or groaning so to be; employing them preferably to others, buying one of another, helping each other in business: and so much the more, because the world will love its own, and them *only.*

By all possible *diligence* and *frugality,* that the gospel be not blamed.

By running with patience the race which is set before them, *denying themselves, and taking up their cross daily;* submitting to bear the reproach of Christ, to be as the filth and offscouring of the world; and looking that men should *say all manner of evil of them falsely, for the Lord's sake.*

(6) It is expected of all who desire to continue in these societies, that they should continue to evidence their desire of salvation.

Thirdly, By attending upon all the ordinances of God: Such are,

The public worship of God:

The ministry of the word, either read or expounded:

The Supper of the Lord:

Family and private prayer:

[Page 102]Searching the scriptures, and Fasting or abstinence.

(7) These are the general rules of our societies: all which we are taught of God to observe, even in his written word, which is the only rule, and

the sufficient rule both of our faith and practice. And all these, we know his Spirit writes on truly awakened hearts. If there be any among us, who observe them not, who habitually break any of them, let it be known unto them who watch over that soul, as they who must give an account. We will admonish him of the error of his ways. We will bear with him for a season. But then, if he repent not, he hath no more place among us. We have delivered our own souls.

SECTION II.

Of Class Meetings.

Quest. 1. How may the leaders of classes be rendered more useful?

Answ. 1. Let each of them be diligently examined concerning his method of meeting a class. Let this be done with all possible exactness, at [Page 103] least once a quarter. In order to this, take sufficient time.

2. Let each leader carefully enquire how every soul in his class prospers: not only how each person observes the outward rules, but how he grows in the knowledge and love of God.

3. Let the leaders converse with those who have the charge of their circuits, frequently and freely.

Quest. 2. Can any thing more be done in order to make the class meetings lively and profitable?

Answ. 1. Change improper leaders.

2. Let the leaders frequently meet each other's classes.

3. Let us observe which leaders are the most useful; and let these meet the other classes as often as possible.

4. See that all the leaders be not only men of sound judgment, but men truly devoted to God.

Quest. 3. How shall we prevent improper persons from insinuating themselves into the society?

Answ. 1. *Give tickets to none until they are recommended by a leader, with*[Page 104]*whom they have met at least six months on trial.*

2. Give notes to none but those who are recommended by one you know, or until they have met three or four times in a class.

3. Read the rules to them the first time they meet.

Quest. 4. How shall we be more exact in receiving and excluding members?

Answ. The official minister or preacher shall, at every quarterly meeting, read the names of those that are received and excluded.

Quest. 5. What shall we do with those members of society, who wilfully and repeatedly neglect to meet their class?

Answ. 1. Let the elder, deacon, or one of the preachers, visit them, whenever it is practicable, and explain to them the consequence if they continue to neglect, viz. Exclusion.

2. If they do not amend, Let him who has the charge of the circuit, exclude them, (in the society), shewing that they are laid aside for a breach of our rules of discipline, and not for immoral conduct.

[Page 105] SECTION III.

Of the Band Societies.

Two, three, or four, true believers, who have confidence in each other, form a Band.—Only it is to be understood, that in one of these Bands all must be men, or all women; and all married, or all unmarried.
[Rules of the Band Societies, drawn up December 25th, 1738.]THE design of our meeting is to obey that command of God, *Confess your faults one to another, and pray one for another, that ye may be healed: Jam.* v. 16.

To this end we agree,

1. To meet once a week, at least.

2. To come punctually at the hour appointed; without some extraordinary reason prevents.

3. To begin exactly at the hour with singing or prayer.

4. To speak, each of us in order, freely and plainly the true state of our souls, with the faults we have committed in tempers, words, or actions, and the temptations we have felt since our last meeting.

5. To end every meeting with [Page 106] prayer, suited to the state of each person present.

6. To desire some person among us to speak *his* own state first, and then to ask the rest in order, as many and as searching questions as may be, concerning their state, sins, and temptations.

Some of the questions proposed to every one, before he is admitted among us, may be to this effect:

1. Have you the forgiveness of your sins?

2. Have you peace with God, through our Lord Jesus Christ?

3. Have you the witness of God's Spirit with your spirit, that you are a child of God?

4. Is the love of God shed abroad in your heart?

5. Has no sin, inward or outward, dominion over you?

6. Do you desire to be told of your faults?

7. Do you desire to be told of *all* your faults, and that plain and home?

8. Do you desire, that every one of us should tell you, from time to time, whatsoever is in our heart concerning you?

[Page 107]9. Consider! Do you desire we should tell you whatsoever we think, whatsoever we fear, whatsoever we hear concerning you?

10. Do you desire, that in doing this, we should come as close as possible, that we should cut to the quick, and search your heart to the bottom?

11. Is it your desire and design, to be on this and all other occasions, entirely open, so as to speak without disguise, and without reserve?

Any of the preceding questions may be asked as often as occasion requires: The four following at every meeting—

1. What known sins have you committed since our last meeting.

2. What particular temptations have you met with?

3. How were you delivered?

4. What have you thought, said, or done, of which you doubt whether it be sin or not?

Directions given to the Band Societies, December 25th, 1744. You are supposed to have the *Faith that overcometh the world*. To you, therefore, it is not grievous,

[Page 108]I. Carefully to abstain from doing evil: in particular,

1. Neither to *buy* nor *sell* any thing at all on the Lord's day.

2. To taste no spirituous liquor, no dram of any kind, unless prescribed by a physician.

3. To be *at a word* both in buying and selling.

4. Not to *mention the fault* of any *behind his back*, and to stop those short that do.

5. To wear no *needless ornaments*, such as rings, ear-rings, neck-laces, lace, ruffles.

6. To use no *needless self-indulgence*.

II. Zealously to maintain good works: in particular,

1. To *give alms* of such things as you possess, and that according to your ability.

2. To reprove those who sin in your sight, and that in love and meekness of wisdom.

3. To be patterns of *diligence* and *frugality,* of *self-denial,* and taking up the cross daily.

III. Constantly to attend on all the ordinances of God: in particular,

[Page 109]1. To be at church, and at the Lord's table, and at every public meeting of the bands, at every opportunity.

2. To use private prayer every day; and family prayer, if you are the head of a family.

3. Frequently to read the scriptures, and meditate thereon. And,

4. To observe, as days of fasting or abstinence, all *Fridays* in the year.

SECTION IV.

Of the privileges granted to serious persons who are not of our society.

Quest. 1. How often shall we permit those who are not of our society, to meet in class or society?

Answ. At every other meeting of the society in every place, let no stranger be admitted. At other times they may; but the same person not above twice or thrice.

Quest. 2. How often shall we permit strangers to be present at our love-feasts?

Answ. Let them be admitted with the utmost caution; and the same [Page 110] person on no account above twice or thrice, unless he become a member.

SECTION V.

Of Marriage.

Quest. 1. Do we observe any evil which has prevailed among our societies with respect to marriage?

Answ. Many of our members have married with *unawakened* persons. This has produced bad effects; they have been either hindered for life, or have turned back to perdition.

Quest. 2. What can be done to discourage this?

Answ. 1. Let every preacher publicly enforce the apostle's caution, "Be ye not unequally yoked together with unbelievers." 2. *Cor.* vi. 14.

2. Let him declare, whoever does this, will be put back on trial six months.

3. When any such is put back on trial, let a suitable exhortation be subjoined.

4. Let all be exhorted to take no step in so weighty a matter, without advising with the most serious of their brethren.

[Page 111]*Quest.* 3. Ought any woman to marry without the consent of her parents?

Answ. In general she ought not. Yet there may be exceptions. For if, 1. A woman believe it to be her duty to marry: If, 2. Her parents absolutely refuse to let her marry any Christian: then she may, nay, ought to marry without their consent. Yet even then a Methodist preacher ought not to be married to her.

We do not prohibit our people from marrying persons who are not of our society, provided such persons have the form, and are seeking the power of godliness; but we are determined to discourage their marrying persons who do not come up to this description. And even in a doubtful case, the member shall be put back on trial.

SECTION VI.

Of Dress.

Quest. SHOULD we insist on the rules concerning dress?

Answ. By all means. This is no time to give any encouragement to [Page 112] superfluity of apparel. Therefore, give no tickets to any, till they have left off superfluous ornaments. In order to this, 1. Let every one who has the charge of a circuit, read the thoughts upon dress, at least once a year in every large society. 2. In visiting the classes, be very mild, but very strict. 3. Allow of no exempt case: Better one suffer than many. 4. Give no tickets to any that wear high heads, enormous bonnets, ruffles, or rings.

SECTION VII.

Of the sale and use of spirituous liquors.

Quest. WHAT directions shall be given concerning the sale and use of spirituous liquors?

Answ. If any member of our society retail or give spirituous liquors, and any thing disorderly be transacted under his roof on this account, the preacher who has the oversight of the circuit shall proceed against him as in the case of other immoralities; and the person accused shall be cleared, censured, suspended or excluded, according to his conduct, as on other charges of immorality.

[Page 113] CHAPTER III. SACRAMENTAL SERVICES, &c.

The Order for the Administration of the Lord's Supper.

The Elder shall say one or more of these sentences.

LET your light so shine before men, that they may see your good works, and glorify your Father who is in heaven. *Matt.* v. 16.

Lay not up for yourselves treasures upon earth, where moth and rust doth corrupt, and where thieves break through and steal: but lay up for yourselves treasures in heaven, where neither moth nor rust doth corrupt, and where thieves do not break through nor steal. *Matt.* vi. 19, 20.

Whatsoever ye would that men should do unto you, even so do unto them; for this is the law and the prophets. *Matt.* vii. 12.

Not every one that saith unto me, Lord, Lord, shall enter into the kingdom of heaven, but he that doeth the will of my Father who is in heaven. *Matt.* vi. 21.

Zaccheus stood forth, and said unto [Page 114] the Lord, Behold, Lord, the half of my goods I give to the poor, and if I have done any wrong to any man, I restore to him fourfold. *Luke* xix. 8.

He that soweth little, shall reap little; and he that soweth plenteously shall reap plenteously. Let every man do according as he is disposed in his heart; not grudgingly, or of necessity: for God loveth a cheerful giver. 2 *Cor.* ix. 6, 7.

While we have time, let us do good unto all men, and especially unto them that are of the household of faith. *Gal.* vi. 10.

Godliness with contentment, is great gain: for we brought nothing into the world, and it is certain we can carry nothing out. 1 *Tim.* vi. 6, 7.

Charge them who are rich in this world, that they be ready to give, and glad to distribute, laying up in store for themselves a good foundation against the time to come, that they may attain eternal life. 1 *Tim.* vi. 17, 18, 19.

God is not unrighteous, that he will forget your works and labour that proceedeth of love; which love ye have shewed for his Name's sake, [Page 115] who have ministered unto the saints, and yet do minister. *Heb.* vi. 10.

To do good, and to distribute, forget not; for with such sacrifices God is well pleased. *Heb.* xiii. 16.

Whoso hath this world's good, and seeth his brother have need, and shutteth up his bowels of compassion from him, how dwelleth the love of God in him? 1 *John* iii. 17.

He that hath pity upon the poor, lendeth unto the Lord; and look, what he layeth out, it shall be paid him again. *Prov.* xix. 17.

Blessed is the man that provideth for the sick and needy: the Lord shall deliver him in time of trouble. *Psalm* xli. 1.

[While these sentences are in reading, some fit person, appointed for that purpose, shall receive the alms for the poor, and other devotions of the people, in a decent bason, to be provided for that purpose: and then bring it to the Elder, who shall place it upon the table.]

After which the Elder shall say,

YE that do truly and earnestly repent of your sins, and are in love and charity with your neighbours, and intend to lead a new life, following [Page 116] the commandments of God, and walking from henceforth in his holy ways; draw near with faith, and take this holy Sacrament to your comfort; and make your humble confession to Almighty God, meekly kneeling upon your knees.

Then shall this general confession be made by the Minister, in the name of all those that are minded to receive the Holy Communion, both he and all the people kneeling humbly upon their knees, and saying.

ALMIGHTY God, Father of our Lord Jesus Christ, Maker of all things, Judge of all men: We acknowledge and bewail our manifold sins and wickedness, which we from time to time most grievously have committed, by thought, word, and deed, against thy Divine Majesty, provoking most justly thy wrath and indignation against us. We do earnestly repent, and are heartily sorry for these our misdoings: The remembrance of them is grievous unto us. Have mercy upon us, have mercy upon us, most merciful Father; for thy Son, our Lord Jesus Christ's sake, forgive us all that is past; and [Page 117] grant that we may ever hereafter serve and please thee in newness of life, to the honour and glory of thy Name, through Jesus Christ our Lord. *Amen.*

Then shall the Elder say,

O ALMIGHTY God, our heavenly Father, who of thy great mercy hast promised forgiveness of sins to all them that with hearty repentance and true faith, turn unto thee; have mercy upon us: pardon and deliver us from all our sins, confirm and strengthen us in all goodness, and bring us to everlasting life, through Jesus Christ our Lord. *Amen.*

The Collect.

ALMIGHTY God, unto whom all hearts be open, all desires known, and from whom no secrets are hid; cleanse the thoughts of our hearts by the inspiration of thy Holy Spirit, that we may perfectly love thee, and worthily magnify thy holy Name, through Christ our Lord. *Amen.*

Then shall the Elder say,

IT is very meet, right, and our bounden duty, that we should at all [Page 118] times, and in all places, give thanks unto thee, O Lord, Holy Father, Almighty, Everlasting God.

Therefore with Angels and Archangels, and with all the company of heaven, we laud and magnify thy glorious Name; evermore praising thee, and saying, Holy, holy, holy, Lord God of Hosts, heaven and earth are full of thy glory. Glory be to thee, O Lord most high. *Amen.*

Then shall the Elder say,

WE do not presume to come to this thy Table, O Merciful Lord, trusting in our own righteousness, but in thy manifold and great mercies. We are not worthy so much as to gather up the crumbs under thy table. But thou art the same Lord, whose property is always to have mercy: Grant us, therefore, gracious Lord, so to eat the flesh of thy dear Son Jesus Christ, and to drink his blood, that our sinful souls and bodies, may be made clean by his death, and washed through his most precious blood; and that we may evermore dwell in him, and he in us. *Amen.*

[Page 119]Then the Elder shall say the prayer of Consecration, as followeth:

ALMIGHTY God, our heavenly Father, who of thy tender mercy, didst give thine only Son, Jesus Christ, to suffer death upon the cross for our redemption; who made there (by his oblation of himself once offered) a full, perfect, and sufficient sacrifice, oblation, and satisfaction for the sins of the whole world; and did institute, and in his holy gospel command us to continue, a perpetual memory of that his precious death, until his coming again: hear us, O Merciful Father, we most humbly beseech thee, and grant that we, receiving these thy creatures of bread and wine, according to thy Son, our Saviour Jesus Christ's holy institution, in remembrance of his death and passion, may be partakers of his most blessed Body and Blood; who, in the same night that he was betrayed, took bread; (1) and when he had given thanks, he brake it (2) and gave it to his disciples, [Page 120] saying, Take eat; this (3) is my Body which is given for you; Do this in remembrance of me. Likewise after supper, he took (4) the cup; and when he had given thanks, he gave it to them, saying, Drink ye all of this; for this (5)

is my blood of the New Testament, which is shed for you, and for many, for the remission of sins; Do this, as oft as ye shall drink it, in remembrance of me. *Amen.* Then shall the Minister first receive the Communion in both kinds himself, and then proceed to deliver the same to the other Ministers in like manner (if any be present) and after that to the people also, in order, into their hands.—And when he delivereth the bread, he shall say,

THE Body of our Lord Jesus Christ, which was given for *thee,* preserve *thy soul* and *body,* unto everlasting life. Take and eat this in [Page 121] remembrance that Christ died for *thee,* and feed on him in *thy heart* by faith with thanksgiving.

And the Minister that delivereth the cup, shall say,

THE Blood of our Lord Jesus Christ, which was shed for *thee,* preserve *thy soul* and *body* unto everlasting life. Drink this in remembrance that Christ's Blood was shed for *thee,* and be thankful.

---

(1) HERE THE ELDER IS TO TAKE THE PLATE OF BREAD INTO HIS HAND.
(2) AND HERE TO BREAK THE BREAD.
(3) AND HERE TO LAY HIS HAND UPON ALL THE BREAD.
(4) HERE HE IS TO TAKE THE CUP IN HIS HAND.
(5) AND HERE TO LAY HIS HAND UPON ALL THE VESSELS WHICH CONTAIN THE WINE.

[If the consecrated Bread or Wine be all spent before all have communicated, the Elder may consecrate more, by repeating the Prayer of Consecration.]

[When all have communicated, the Minister shall return to the Lord's Table, and place upon it what remaineth of the consecrated elements, covering the same with a fair Linen Cloth.]

Then shall the Elder say the Lord's Prayer, the people repeating after him every petition.

OUR Father, who art in Heaven, Hallowed be thy Name; Thy Kingdom come: Thy will be done on earth as it is in heaven; give us this day our daily bread; and forgive us our trespasses, as we forgive them that trespass against us: And lead us not into temptation, but deliver us [Page 122] from evil, for thine is the Kingdom, and the Power, and the Glory, for ever and ever. *Amen.*

After which shall be said as followeth:

O LORD and heavenly Father, we thy humble servants, desire thy Fatherly goodness, mercifully to accept this our sacrifice of praise and thanksgiving; most humbly beseeching thee to grant, that by the merits and death of thy Son Jesus Christ, and through faith in his blood, we and thy whole church, may obtain remission of our sins, and all other benefits of his passion. And here we offer and present unto thee, O Lord, ourselves, our souls and bodies, to be a reasonable, holy, and lively sacrifice unto thee; humbly beseeching thee that all we who are partakers of this holy Communion, may be filled with thy grace and heavenly benediction. And although we be unworthy, through our manifold sins, to offer unto thee any sacrifice, yet we beseech thee to accept this our bounden duty and service; not weighing our merits, but pardoning [Page 123] our offences, through Jesus Christ our Lord: by whom, and with whom, in the unity of the Holy Ghost, all honour and glory be unto thee, O Father Almighty, world without end. *Amen.*

Then shall be said,

GLORY be to God on high, and on earth peace, good will towards men. We praise thee, we bless thee, we worship thee, we glorify thee, we give thanks to thee for thy great glory, O Lord God, heavenly King, God the Father Almighty.

O Lord, the only begotten Son Jesus Christ; O Lord God, Lamb of God, Son of the Father, that takest away the sins of the world, have mercy upon us. Thou that takest away the sins of the world, have mercy upon us. Thou that takest away the sins of the world, receive our prayer. Thou that sittest at the right hand of God the Father, have mercy upon us.

For thou only art holy, thou only art the Lord, thou only, O Christ, with the Holy Ghost, art most high in the glory of God the Father. *Amen.*

[Page 124]Then the Elder, if he see it expedient, may put up an ex tempore Prayer: and afterwards shall let the people depart with this blessing:

MAY the peace of God, which passeth all understanding, keep your hearts and minds in the knowledge and love of God, and of his Son Jesus Christ our Lord; and the blessing of God Almighty, the Father, the Son, and the Holy Ghost, be amongst you, and remain with you always. *Amen.*

N. B. If the Elder be straitened for time, he may omit any part of the service, except the prayer of Consecration.

The Ministration of BAPTISM of Infants.

The Minister coming to the font, which is to be filled with pure water, shall use the following, or some other exhortation suitable to this sacred Office:

DEARLY beloved, forasmuch as all men are conceived and born in sin, and that our Saviour Christ saith, None can enter into the kingdom of God, except he be regenerate and born anew of water and of the Holy [Page 125] Ghost: I beseech you to call upon God the Father, through our Lord Jesus Christ, that of his bounteous mercy he will grant to *this Child* that thing which by nature *he* cannot have; that *he* may be baptized with water, and the Holy Ghost, and received into Christ's holy church, and be made a *lively member* of the same.

Then shall the Minister say,

Let us pray.

ALMIGHTY and everlasting God, who of thy great mercy, didst save Noah and his family in the ark from perishing by water; and also didst safely lead the children of Israel, thy people, through the Red Sea, figuring thereby thy holy baptism: and by the baptism of thy well beloved Son Jesus Christ in the river Jordan, didst sanctify water for this holy sacrament, we beseech thee, for thine infinite mercies, that thou wilt look upon *this child*: wash *him* and sanctify *him* with the Holy Ghost; that *he* being delivered from thy wrath, may be received into the ark of Christ's church, and being [Page 126] stedfast in faith, joyful through hope, and rooted in love, may so pass the waves of this troublesome world, that finally *he* may come to the land of everlasting life; there to reign with thee, world without end, through Jesus Christ our Lord. *Amen.*

O MERCIFUL God, grant that the old Adam in *this child,* may be so buried, that the new man may be raised up in *him. Amen.*

GRANT that all carnal affections may die in *him,* and that all things belonging to the Spirit may live and grow in *him. Amen.*

GRANT that *he* may have power and strength to have victory, and to triumph against the devil, the world, and the flesh. *Amen.*

GRANT that whosoever is dedicated to thee by our Office and Ministry, may also be endued with heavenly virtues, and everlastingly rewarded through thy mercy, O blessed Lord God, who dost live and govern all things, world without end. *Amen.*

ALMIGHTY everliving God, whose most dearly beloved Son Jesus Christ, [Page 127] for the forgiveness of our sins, did shed out of his most precious side, both water and blood, and gave commandment to his disciples that they should go teach all nations, and baptize them in the Name of the Father, and of the Son, and of the Holy Ghost, regard we beseech thee, the supplications of thy congregation; sanctify this water for this holy Sacrament; and grant that *this child,* now to be baptized, may receive the fulness of thy grace, and ever remain in the number of thy faithful and elect children, through Jesus Christ our Lord. *Amen.*

Then shall the people stand up; and the Minister shall say,
Hear the words of the Gospel written by St. Mark, in the tenth chapter, at the thirteenth verse.

THEY brought young children to Christ, that he should touch them. And his disciples rebuked those that brought them; but when Jesus saw it he was much displeased, and said unto them, Suffer the little children to come unto me, and forbid them not, for of such is the kingdom of [Page 128] God. Verily, I say unto you, Whosoever shall not receive the kingdom of God as a little child, he shall not enter therein. And he took them up in his arms, put his hands upon them, and blessed them.

Then the Minister shall take the Child into his hands, and say to the friends of the Child,
Name this Child.

And then, naming it after them, he shall sprinkle or pour water upon it, or if desired, immerse it in water, saying,

N. I baptize thee, in the name of the Father, and of the Son, and of the Holy Ghost. *Amen.*

Then shall be said, all kneeling,

OUR Father, who art in Heaven, hallowed be thy Name; Thy Kingdom come; Thy will be done on earth, as it is in Heaven: Give us this day our daily bread; and forgive us our trespasses, as we forgive them that trespass against us: And lead us not into temptation; but deliver us from evil. *Amen.*

[Then shall the Minister conclude with extemporary prayer.]

[Page 129] *The Ministration of BAPTISM to such as are of Riper Years.*

The Minister shall use the following, or some other exhortation, suitable to this holy office.

DEARLY beloved, forasmuch as all men are conceived and born in sin, (and that which is born of the flesh is flesh, and they that are in the flesh cannot please God, but live in sin, committing many actual transgressions:) and that our Saviour Christ saith, None can enter into the kingdom of God, except he be regenerate, and born anew of water and of the Holy Ghost: I beseech you to call upon God the Father, through our Lord Jesus Christ, that of his bounteous goodness he will grant to *these persons,* that which by nature *they* cannot have; that *they* may be baptized with water and the Holy Ghost, and received into Christ's holy church, and he made *lively members* of the same.

Then shall the Minister say,

ALMIGHTY and immortal God, the aid of all that need, the helper [Page 130] of all that flee to thee for succour, the life of them that believe, and the resurrection of the dead; We call upon thee for *these persons; that they,* coming to thy holy baptism, may receive remission of their sins by spiritual regeneration. Receive *them,* O Lord, as thou hast promised by thy well-beloved Son, saying, Ask, and ye shall receive; seek, and ye shall find; knock, and it shall be opened unto you: So give now unto us that ask; let us that seek find; open the gate unto us that knock; that *these persons* may enjoy the everlasting benediction of thy heavenly washing, and may come to the eternal kingdom which thou hast promised by Christ our Lord. *Amen.*

After which he shall say,

ALMIGHTY and everlasting God, heavenly Father, we give thee humble thanks, for that thou hast vouchsafed to call us to the knowledge of thy grace, and faith in thee; increase this knowledge and confirm this faith in us evermore. Give thy Holy Spirit to *these persons,* that [Page 131]*they* may be born again, and be made *heirs* of everlasting salvation, through our

Lord Jesus Christ, who liveth and reigneth with thee and the Holy Spirit, now and for ever. *Amen.*

Then shall the people stand up, and the Minister shall say,
Hear the words of the Gospel written by St. John, in the third chapter, beginning at the first verse.

THERE was a man of the Pharisees, named Nicodemus, a ruler of the Jews: the same came to Jesus by night, and said unto him, Rabbi, we know that thou art a teacher come from God; for no man can do these miracles that thou doest, except God be with him. Jesus answered and said unto him, Verily, verily, I say unto thee, Except a man be born again, he cannot see the kingdom of God. Nicodemus saith unto him, How can a man be born when he is old? Can he enter the second time into his mother's womb, and be born? Jesus answered, Verily, verily, I say unto thee, Except a man be born of water and [Page 132] of the Spirit, he cannot enter into the kingdom of God. That which is born of the flesh is flesh, and that which is born of the Spirit is spirit. Marvel not that I said unto thee, Ye must be born again. The wind bloweth where it listeth, and thou hearest the sound thereof; but canst not tell whence it cometh, and whither it goeth: so is every one that is born of the Spirit.

Then the Minister shall speak to the persons to be baptized, on this wise:

WELL beloved, who *are* come hither, desiring to receive holy Baptism, *ye* have heard how the congregation hath prayed, that our Lord Jesus Christ would vouchsafe to receive you, and bless you, to release you of your sins, to give you the kingdom of heaven, and everlasting life. And our Lord Jesus Christ hath promised in his holy word, to grant all those things that we have prayed for: which promise he for his part will most surely keep and perform.

Wherefore, after this promise made by Christ, *you* must also faithfully, for *your* part, promise in the presence [Page 133] of this whole congregation, that you will renounce the devil and all his works, and constantly believe God's holy word, and obediently keep his commandments.

Then shall the Minister demand of each of the persons to be baptized, severally,

Quest. DOST thou renounce the devil and all his works, the vain pomp and glory of the world, with all covetuous desires of the same, and the carnal desires of the flesh, so that thou wilt not follow, or be led by them?

Answ. I renounce them all.

Quest. DOST thou believe in God, the Father Almighty, Maker of heaven and earth? And in Jesus Christ his only begotten Son, our Lord? And that he was conceived by the Holy Ghost, born of the Virgin Mary? That he suffered under Pontius Pilate, was crucified, dead, and buried; that he rose again the third day; that he ascended into heaven, and sitteth at the right hand of God the Father Almighty; and from thence shall come again, at [Page 134] the end of the world, to judge the quick and the dead:

And dost thou believe in the Holy Ghost; the Holy Catholic Church; the Communion of Saints; the Remission of Sins; the Resurrection of the Body; and everlasting life after death?

Answ. All this I stedfastly believe.

Quest. WILT thou be baptized in this faith?

Answ. This is my desire.

Quest. WILT thou then obediently keep God's holy will and commandments, and walk in the same all the days of thy life?

Answ. I will endeavour so to do, God being my helper.

Then shall the Minister say,

O MERCIFUL God, grant that the old Adam in *these persons*, may be so buried, that the new man may be raised up in *them*. *Amen.*

GRANT that all carnal affections may die in *them*, and that all things belonging to the Spirit may live and grow in *them*. *Amen.*

[Page 135]GRANT that they may have power and strength to have victory, and triumph against the devil, the world, and the flesh. *Amen.*

GRANT that *they* being here dedicated to thee by our Office and Ministry, may also be endued with heavenly virtues, and everlastingly rewarded, through thy mercy, O blessed Lord God, who dost live and govern all things, world without end. *Amen.*

ALMIGHTY everliving God, whose most dearly beloved Son Jesus Christ, for the forgiveness of our sins, did shed out of his most precious side, both water and blood; and gave commandment to his disciples, that they should go teach all nations, and baptize them in the name of the Father, and of the Son, and of the Holy Ghost: Regard, we beseech thee, the supplications of this congregation; and grant that the *persons* now to be baptized, may receive the fulness of thy grace, and ever remain in the number of thy faithful and elect children, through Jesus Christ our Lord. *Amen.*

[Page 136]Then shall the Minister take each person to be baptized by the right hand, and placing him conveniently by the font, according to his discretion, shall ask the name; and then shall sprinkle or pour water upon him (or if he shall desire it, shall immerse him in water) saying,

N: I baptize thee in the Name of the Father, and of the Son, and of the Holy Ghost. *Amen.*

Then shall be said the Lord's Prayer, all kneeling:

OUR Father, who art in Heaven, Hallowed be thy Name; thy Kingdom come; thy will be done on earth as it is in Heaven: Give us this day our daily bread; and forgive us our trespasses, as we forgive them that trespass against us: And lead us not into temptation, but deliver us from evil. *Amen.*

[Then let the Minister conclude with extemporary Prayer]

[Page 137] *The form of Solemnization of Matrimony.*

First, the Banns of all that are to be married together, must be published in the congregation, three several Sundays, in the time of Divine Service (unless they be otherwise qualified according to law) the Minister saying after the accustomed manner,

I PUBLISH the Banns of marriage between *M* of _____, and *N* of _____. If any of you know cause or just impediment why these two persons should not be joined together in holy Matrimony, *ye* are to declare it. This is the first, (*second,* or *third*) time of asking.

At the day and time appointed for Solemnization of Matrimony, the Persons to be married, standing together, the Man on the right hand, and the Woman on the left, the Minister shall say,

DEARLY beloved, we are gathered together here, in the sight of God, and in the presence of these witnesses, to join together this man and this woman in holy Matrimony: which is an honourable estate, instituted of God in the time of man's innocence, signifying unto us the [Page 138] mystical union that is betwixt Christ and his Church; which holy estate Christ adorned and beautified with his presence, and first miracle that he wrought in Cana of Galilee, and is commended of St. Paul to be honourable among all men; and therefore is not by any to be enterprised or taken in hand unadvisedly, but reverently, discreetly, advisedly, and in the fear of God.

Into which holy estate these two persons present come now to be joined. Therefore if any can shew any just cause why they way not lawfully be joined together, let him now speak, or else hereafter for ever hold his peace.

And also speaking unto the persons that are to be married, he shall say,

I REQUIRE and charge you both (as you will answer at the dreadful day of judgment, when the secrets of all hearts shall be disclosed) that if either of you know any impediment why you may not be lawfully joined together in matrimony, you do now confess it. For be ye well assured, [Page 139] that so many as are coupled together otherwise than God's word doth allow, are not joined together by God, neither is their matrimony lawful.

If no impediment be alledged, then shall the Minister say unto the Man,

M. WILT thou have this Woman to thy wedded Wife, to live together after God's ordinance, in the holy estate of Matrimony? Wilt thou love her, comfort her, honour and keep her, in sickness and in health; and forsaking all other, keep thee only unto her, so long as ye both shall live?

The Man shall answer,

I will.

Then shall the Minister say unto the Woman, *N.* WILT thou have this Man to thy wedded husband, to live together after God's ordinance, in the holy estate of Matrimony? Wilt thou obey him, serve him, love, honour and keep him, in sickness and in health; and forsaking all other, keep thee only unto him, so long as ye both shall live?

The Woman shall answer,

I will.

[Page 140]Then the Minister shall cause the Man with his right hand to take the Woman by her right hand, and to say after him as followeth:

I *M*, take thee *N*, to be my wedded Wife, to have and to hold, from this day forward, for better, for worse, for richer, for poorer, in sickness and in health, to love and to cherish, till death us do part, according to God's holy ordinance; and thereto I plight thee my faith.

Then shall they loose their hands, and the Woman with her right hand, taking the Man by his right hand, shall likewise say after the Minister,

I *N*, take thee *M*, to be my wedded Husband, to have and to hold, from this day forward, for better, for worse, for richer, for poorer, in sickness and in health, to love, cherish, and to obey, till death do us part, according to God's holy ordinance; and thereto I give thee my faith.

Then shall the Minister say,

Let us pray.

O ETERNAL God, Creator and Preserver of all mankind, Giver of [Page 141] all Spiritual grace, the Author of everlasting life; send thy blessing upon these thy servants, this Man and this Woman, whom we bless in thy Name; that as Isaac and Rebecca lived faithfully together, so these persons may surely perform and keep the vow and covenant betwixt them made, and may ever remain in perfect love and peace together, and live according to thy laws, through Jesus Christ our Lord. *Amen.*

Then shall the Minister join their right hands together and say,

Those whom God hath joined together, let no man put asunder.

FORASMUCH as *M,* and *N,* have consented together in holy wedlock, and have witnessed the same before God and this company, and thereto have pledged their faith either to other, and have declared the same by joining of hands: I pronounce that they are Man and Wife together, in the name of the Father, and of the Son, and of the Holy Ghost. *Amen.*

[Page 142]And the Minister shall add this blessing:

GOD the Father, God the Son, God the Holy Ghost, bless, preserve, and keep you; the Lord mercifully with his favour look upon you, and so fill you with all spiritual benediction and grace; that ye may so live together in this life, that in the world to come ye may have life everlasting. *Amen.*

Then the Minister shall say,

OUR Father, who art in heaven, Hallowed by thy Name: Thy kingdom come: Thy will be done on earth, as it is in heaven: Give us this day our daily bread; And forgive us our trespasses, as we forgive them that trespass against us: And lead us not into temptation; But deliver us from evil. *Amen.*

Then shall the Minister say,

O GOD of Abraham, God of Isaac, God of Jacob, bless this man and this woman, and sow the seed of eternal life in their hearts, that whatsoever in thy holy Word they shall profitably learn, they may in deed [Page 143] fulfil the same. Look, O Lord, mercifully upon them from heaven, and bless them. And as thou didst send thy blessing upon Abraham and Sarah, to their great comfort; so vouchsafe to send thy blessing upon this man and this woman; that they obeying thy will, and always being in safety under thy protection, may abide in thy love unto their lives end, through Jesus Christ our Lord. *Amen.*

O GOD, who by thy mighty power hast made all things of nothing, who also (after other things set in order) didst appoint that out of man (created after thine own image and similitude) woman should take her beginning: and knitting them together, didst teach that it should never be lawful to put asunder those whom thou by Matrimony hadst made one; O God, who hast consecrated the state of Matrimony to such an excellent mystery, that in it is signified and represented the spiritual marriage and unity betwixt Christ and his Church: Look mercifully upon this man and this woman;

[Page 144] that both this man may love his wife, according to thy word (as Christ did love his Spouse the Church, who gave himself for it; loving and cherishing it, even as his own flesh) and also that this woman may be loving and amiable, faithful and obedient to her husband: and in all quietness, sobriety, and peace, be a follower of holy and godly matrons. O Lord, bless them both, and grant them to inherit thy everlasting kingdom, through Jesus Christ our Lord. *Amen.*

Then shall the Minister say,

ALMIGHTY God, who at the beginning did create our first parents, Adam and Eve, and did sanctify and join them together in marriage, pour upon you the riches of his grace, sanctify and bless you, that ye may please him both in body and soul, and live together in holy love unto your lives end. *Amen.*

[Page 145] *The Order of the Burial of the Dead.*

N.B. The following or some other solemn service shall be used.
The Minister meeting the Corpse, and going before it, shall say,

I AM the resurrection and the life, saith the Lord: he that believeth in me, though he were dead, yet shall he live: and whosoever liveth and believeth in me, shall never die. *John* xi. 25, 26.

I KNOW that my Redeemer liveth, and that he shall stand at the latter day upon the earth. And though after my skin, worms destroy this body, yet in my flesh shall I see God: whom I shall see for myself, and mine eyes shall behold, and not another. *Job* xix. 25, 26, 27.

WE brought nothing into this world, and it is certain we can carry nothing out. The Lord gave, and the Lord hath taken away; blessed be the Name of the Lord. 1 *Tim.* vi. 7. *Job* i. 21.

At the Grave, when the Corpse is laid in the earth, the Minister shall say,

MAN that is born of a woman hath [Page 146] but a short time to live, and is full of misery. He cometh up, and is cut down like a flower: he fleeth as it were a shadow, and never continueth in one stay.

In the midst of life we are in death: of whom may we seek for succour, but of thee, O Lord, who for our sins art justly displeased?

Yet, O Lord God most holy, O Lord most mighty, O holy and most merciful Saviour, deliver us not into the bitter pains of eternal death.

Thou knowest, Lord, the secrets of our hearts: shut not thy merciful ears to our prayers, but spare us, Lord most holy, O God most mighty, O holy and merciful Saviour, thou most worthy Judge eternal, suffer us not at our last hour, for any pains of death to fall from thee.

Then shall be said,

I HEARD a voice from heaven, saying unto me, Write; From henceforth blessed are the dead who die in the Lord: even so saith the Spirit: for they rest from their labours.

[Page 147] Then shall the Minister say,

Lord have mercy upon us.
Christ have mercy upon us.
Lord have mercy upon us.

OUR Father, who art in Heaven, hallowed be thy Name: Thy Kingdom come: Thy will be done on earth, as it is in Heaven: Give us this day our daily bread; and forgive us our trespasses, as we forgive them that trespass against us: And lead us not into temptation; but deliver us from evil. *Amen.*

The Collect.

O MERCIFUL God, the Father of our Lord Jesus Christ, who is the resurrection and the life; in whom whosoever believeth shall live, though he die: and whosoever liveth and believeth in him, shall not die eternally: We meekly beseech thee, O Father, to raise us from the death of sin unto the life of righteousness; that when we shall depart this life, we may rest in him; and at the general resurrection on the last day, may be found acceptable in thy sight, and receive that blessing which thy [Page 148] well-beloved Son shall then pronounce to all that love and fear thee, saying, Come ye blessed children of my Father, receive the kingdom prepared for you from the beginning of the world. Grant this, be beseech thee, O merciful Father, through Jesus Christ our Mediator and Redeemer. *Amen.*

THE grace of our Lord Jesus Christ, and the love of God, and the fellowship of the Holy Ghost, be with us all evermore. *Amen.*

THE FORM AND MANNER OF MAKING AND ORDAINING OF BISHOPS, ELDERS, AND DEACONS.

The Form and Manner of Making of Deacons.

[When the day appointed by the Bishop is come, there shall be a sermon, or exhortation, declaring the duty and office of such as come to be admitted Deacons.]

After which, one of the Elders shall present unto the Bishop the persons to be ordained [Page 149] Deacons: and their names being read aloud, the Bishop shall say unto the people:

BRETHREN, if there be any of you, who knoweth any impediment or crime in any of these persons presented to be ordained Deacons, for the which he ought not to be admitted to that office, let him come forth in the name of God, and shew what the crime or impediment is.

[If any crime or impediment be objected, the Bishop shall surcease from ordaining that person, until such time as the party accused shall be found clear of that crime.]

Then shall be read the following Collect and Epistle.

The Collect.

ALMIGHTY God, who by thy divine Providence hast appointed divers orders of ministers in thy church, and didst inspire thy apostles to choose into the order of Deacons, thy first martyr St. Stephen, with others: Mercifully behold these thy servants now called to the like office and administration: replenish them so with the truth of thy doctrine, and adorn them with innocency [Page 150] of life, that both by word and good example, they may faithfully serve thee in this office, to the glory of thy name, and the edification of thy church, through the merits of our Saviour Jesus Christ, who liveth and reigneth with thee and the Holy Ghost, now and for ever. *Amen*

The Epistle. 1 *Tim.* iii. 8—13.

LIKEWISE must the Deacons be grave, not double-tongued, not given to much wine, not greedy of filthy lucre; holding the mystery of the faith in a pure conscience. And let these also first be proved, then let them use the office of a Deacon, being found blameless. Even so must their wives be grave, not slanderers, sober, faithful in all things. Let the Deacons be the husbands of one wife, ruling their children and their own houses well. For they that have used the office of a deacon well, purchase to themselves a good degree, and great boldness in the faith which is in Christ Jesus.

[Page 151]Then shall the Bishop examine every one that is to be ordained, in the presence of the People, after this manner following:

Do you trust that you are inwardly moved by the Holy Ghost, to take upon you the office of the ministry in the church of Christ, to serve God for the promoting of his glory, and the edifying of his people?

Answ. I trust so.

The Bishop. Do you unfeignedly believe all the canonical Scriptures of the Old and New Testament?

Answ. I do believe them.

The Bishop. WILL you diligently read or expound the same unto the people whom you shall be appointed to serve?

Answ. I will.

The Bishop. IT appertaineth to the office of a Deacon to assist the Elder in Divine Service. And especially, when he ministereth the holy communion to help him in the distribution thereof, and to read and expound the holy Scriptures; to instruct the youth; and in the absence of the Elder, to baptize. And furthermore, it is his office, to search for [Page 152] the sick, poor, and impotent, that they may be visited and relieved. Will you do this gladly and willingly?

Answ. I will do so, by the help of God.

The Bishop. WILL you apply all your diligence to frame and fashion your own lives (and the lives of your families) according to the doctrine of Christ; and to make (both) yourselves (and them) as much as in you lieth, wholesome examples of the flock of Christ?

Answ. I will do so, the Lord being my helper.

The Bishop. WILL you reverently obey them to whom the charge and government over you is committed, following with a glad mind and will, their godly admonitions?

Answ. I will endeavour so to do, the Lord being my helper.

Then the Bishop laying his hands severally upon the Head of every one of them, shall say,

TAKE thou authority to execute the Office of a Deacon in the church of God; in the Name of the Father, [Page 153] and of the Son, and of the Holy Ghost. *Amen.*

Then shall the Bishop deliver to every one of them the Holy Bible, saying,

TAKE thou authority to read the holy Scriptures in the church of God, and to preach the same.

Then one of them appointed by the Bishop, shall read the Gospel. Luke xii. 35—38.

LET your loins be girded about, and your lights burning, and ye yourselves like unto men that wait for their Lord, when he will return from the wedding, that when he cometh and knocketh, they may open unto him immediately. Blessed are those servants, whom the Lord when he cometh shall find watching. Verily I say unto you, That he shall gird himself, and make them to sit down to meat, and will come forth and serve them. And if he shall come in the second watch, or come in the third watch, and find them so, blessed are those servants.

[Page 154][Then shall the Bishop proceed in the communion, and all that are ordained shall receive the holy communion.]

The communion ended, immediately before the Benediction, shall be said these Collects following:

ALMIGHTY God, giver of all good things, who of thy great goodness, hast vouchsafed to accept and take these thy servants into the office of Deacons in thy church: Make them, we beseech thee, O Lord, to be modest, humble, and constant in their ministration, and to have a ready will to observe all spiritual discipline; that they having always the testimony of a good conscience, and continuing ever stable and strong in thy Son Christ, may so well behave themselves in this inferior office, that they may be found worthy to be called unto the higher ministries in thy church, through the same thy Son our Saviour Jesus Christ; to whom be glory and honour, world without end. *Amen.*

PREVENT us, O Lord, in all our doings, with thy most gracious favour, and further us with thy continual [Page 155] help; that in all our works begun, continued and ended in thee, we may glorify thy holy Name, and finally by thy mercy, obtain everlasting life, through Jesus Christ our Lord. *Amen.*

THE peace of God, which passeth all understanding, keep your hearts and minds in the knowledge and love of God, and of his Son Jesus Christ our Lord; and the blessing of God Almighty, the Father, the Son, and the Holy Ghost, be amongst you, and remain with you always. *Amen.*

The Form and Manner of Ordaining of Elders.

[When the day appointed by the Bishop is come, there shall be a Sermon or Exhortation, declaring the Duty and Office of such as come to be admitted Elders; how necessary that order is in the Church of Christ, and also how the people ought to esteem them in their office.]

After which, one of the Elders shall present unto the Bishop all them that are to be ordained, and say,

I PRESENT unto you these persons present, to be ordained Elders.

[Page 156]Then their Names being read aloud, the Bishop shall say unto the People,

BRETHREN, these are they whom we purpose, God willing, this day to ordain Elders. For after due examination, we find not to the contrary, but that they are lawfully called to this function and ministry, and that they are persons meet for the same. But if there be any of you, who knoweth any impediment or crime in any of them, for the which he ought not to be received into this holy ministry, let him come forth in the name of God, and shew what the crime or impediment is.

[If any crime or impediment be objected, the Bishop shall surcease from ordaining that Person, until such time as the party accused shall be found clear of the crime.]

Then shall be said the Collect, Epistle, and Gospel, as followeth.

The Collect.

ALMIGHTY God, giver of all good things, who by thy Holy Spirit hast [Page 157] appointed divers orders of ministers in thy church; Mercifully behold these thy servants, now called to the office of Elders, and replenish them so with the truth of thy doctrine, and adorn them with innocency of life, that both by word and good example they may faithfully serve thee in this office, to the glory of thy name, and the edification of thy church, through the merits of our Saviour Jesus Christ, who liveth and reigneth with thee and the Holy Ghost, world without end. *Amen.*

The Epistle. Eph. iv. 7—13.

UNTO every one of us is given grace according to the measure of the gift of Christ. Wherefore he saith, When he ascended up on high he led captivity captive, and gave gifts unto men. (Now that he ascended, what is it but that he also descended first, into the lower parts of the earth? He that descended, is the same also that ascended up far above all heavens, that he might fill all things.) And he gave some Apostles; and some prophets;

and some [Page 158] evangelists; and some pastors and teachers; for the perfecting of the saints, for the work of the ministry, for the edifying of the body of Christ, till we all come in the unity of the faith, and of the knowledge of the Son of God, unto a perfect man, unto the measure of the stature of the fulness of Christ.

After this shall be read for the Gospel, part of the tenth chapter of St. John.

St. John x. 1—16.

VERILY, verily, I say unto you, He that entereth not by the door into the sheep-fold, but climbeth up some other way, the same is a thief and a robber. But he that entereth in by the door, is the shepherd of the sheep. To him the porter openeth, and the sheep hear his voice, and he calleth his own sheep by name, and leadeth them out. And when he putteth forth his own sheep, he goeth before them, and the sheep follow him, for they know his voice. And a stranger will they not follow, but fiee from him; for they know not the voice of strangers. This parable [Page 159] spake Jesus unto them, but they understood not what things they were which he spake unto them. Then said Jesus unto them again, Verily, verily, I say unto you, I am the door of the sheep. All that ever came before me are thieves and robbers, but the sheep did not hear them. I am the door; by me if any man enter in, he shall be saved, and shall go in and out, and find pasture. The thief cometh not but for to steal, and to kill, and to destroy: I am come that they might have life, and that they might have it more abundantly. I am the good Shepherd: the good shepherd giveth his life for the sheep. But he that is an hireling, and not the Shepherd, whose own the sheep are not, seeth the wolf coming, and leaveth the sheep, and fleeth, and the wolf catcheth them, and scattereth the sheep. The hireling fleeth because he is an hireling, and careth not for the sheep. I am the good Shepherd, and know my sheep, and am known of mine. As the Father knoweth me, even so know I the Father: and I lay down my life for the [Page 160] sheep. And other sheep I have which are not of this fold: them also I must bring, and they shall hear my voice, and there shall be one fold and one Shepherd.

And that done, the Bishop shall say unto them as hereafter followeth:

You have heard, brethren, as well in your private examination, as in the exhortation which was now made to you, and in the holy lessons taken out of the Gospel, and the writings of the Apostles, of what dignity, and of how great importance this office is, whereunto you are called. And now again we exhort you in the name of our Lord Jesus Christ, that you have in remembrance, into how high a dignity, and to how weighty an office ye are called: That is to say, to be messengers, watchmen, and stewards of the Lord, to teach, and to premonish, to feed and provide for the Lord's family, to seek for Christ's sheep that are dispersed abroad, and for his children who are in the midst of this evil world, that they may be saved through Christ for ever.

[Page 161]Have always, therefore, printed in your remembrance, how great a treasure is committed to your charge. For they are the sheep of Christ, which he bought with his death, and for whom he shed his blood. The church and congregation whom you must serve, is his Spouse, and his body. And if it shall happen, the same church, or any member thereof, do take any hurt or hindrance by reason of your negligence, ye know the greatness of the fault, and also the horrible punishment that will ensue. Wherefore, consider with yourselves the end of the ministry towards the children of God, towards the Spouse and body of Christ; and see that you never cease your labour, your care and diligence, until you have done all that lieth in you, according to your bounden duty, to bring all such as are or shall be committed to your charge, unto that agreement in the faith and knowledge of God, and to that ripeness and perfectness of age in Christ, that there be no place left among you, either for error in religion, or for viciousness in life.

[Page 162]Forasmuch then as your office is both of so great excellency, and of so great difficulty, ye see with how great care and study ye ought to apply yourselves, as well that ye may show yourselves dutiful and thankful unto that Lord, who bath placed you in so high a dignity; as also to beware that neither you yourselves offend, nor be occasion that others offend. Howbeit ye cannot have a mind and will thereto of yourselves: for that will and ability is given of God alone; therefore ye ought, and have need to pray earnestly for his Holy Spirit. And seeing that ye cannot by any other means compass the doing of so weighty a work, pertaining to the salvation of man, but with doctrine and exhortation taken out of the holy Scriptures, and with a life agreeable to the same: consider how studious ye ought to be in reading and learning the Scriptures, and in framing the manners both of yourselves and of them that specially pertain unto you, according to the rule of the same Scriptures; and this self-same cause, how ye ought to forsake [Page 163] and set aside (as much as you may) all worldly cares and studies.

We have good hope that you have all weighed and pondered these things with yourselves long before this time; and that you have clearly determined, by God's grace, to give yourselves wholly to this office, whereunto it hath pleased God to call you: so that, as much as lieth in you, you will apply yourselves wholly to this one thing, and draw all your cares and studies this way, and that you will continually pray to God the Father, by the mediation of our only Saviour Jesus Christ, for the heavenly assistance of the Holy Ghost; that by daily reading and weighing of the Scriptures, ye may wax riper and stronger in your ministry; and that ye may so endeavour, yourselves, from time to time, to sanctify the lives of you and your's, and to fashion them after the rule and doctrine of Christ, that ye may be wholesome and godly examples and patterns for the people to follow.

And now that this present congregation of Christ, here assembled, may [Page 164] also understand your minds and wills in these things, and that this your promise may the more move you to do your duties: ye shall answer plainly to these things which we, in the name of God and his Church, shall demand of you touching the same.

Do you think in your heart, that you are truly called, according to the will of our Lord Jesus Christ, to the order of Elders?

Answ. I think so.

The Bishop. ARE you persuaded that the Holy Scriptures contain sufficiently all doctrine required of necessity for eternal salvation through faith in Jesus Christ? And are you determined, out of the said Scriptures to instruct the people committed to your charge, and to teach nothing as required of necessity to eternal salvation, but that which you shall be persuaded, may be concluded and proved by the Scripture?

Answ. I am so persuaded, and have so determined, by God's grace

The Bishop. WILL you then give your faithful diligence, always so to minister the doctrine and sacraments, [Page 165] and discipline of Christ, as the Lord hath commanded?

Answ. I will so do, by the help of the Lord.

The Bishop. WILL you be ready with all faithful diligence to banish and drive away all erroneous and strange doctrines contrary to God's word; and to use both public and private monitions and exhortations, as well to the sick, as to the whole, within your district, as need shall require, and occasion shall be given?

Answ. I will, the Lord being my helper.

The Bishop. WILL you be diligent in prayers, and in reading of the holy Scriptures, and in such studies as help to the knowledge of the same, laying aside the study of the world and the flesh?

Answ. I will endeavour so to do, the Lord being my helper.

The Bishop. WILL you be diligent to frame and fashion your own selves, and your families, according to the doctrine of Christ; and to make both yourselves and them, as much as in you lieth, wholesome examples and patterns to the flock of Christ?

[Page 166]*Answ.* I shall apply myself thereto, the Lord being my helper.

The Bishop. WILL you maintain and set forward, as much as lieth in you, quietness, peace, and love among all Christian People, and especially among them that are or shall be committed to your charge?

Answ. I will so do, the Lord being my helper.

The Bishop. WILL you reverently obey your chief ministers, unto whom is committed the charge and government over you; following with a glad mind and will their godly admonitions, submitting yourselves to their godly judgments?

Answ. I will so do, the Lord being my helper.

Then shall the Bishop, standing up, say,

ALMIGHTY God, who hath given you this will to do all these things, grant also unto you strength and power to perform the same; that he may accomplish his work which be hath begun in you, through Jesus Christ our Lord. *Amen.*

[Page 167][After this the Congregation shall be desired secretly in their prayers, to make their humble supplications to God for all these things: for the which prayers there shall be silence kept for a space.]

After which shall be said by the Bishop, (the Persons to be ordained Elders all kneeling) VENI, CREATOR SPIRITUS, the Bishop beginning, and the Elders and others, that are present, answering by verse, as followeth:

COME, Holy Ghost, our souls inspire,
And lighten with celestial fire.
Thou the anointing Spirit art,
Who dost thy sev'n-fold gifts impart.
Thy blessed Unction from above
Is comfort, life, and fire of love.
Enable with perpetual light
The dulness of our blinded sight;

Anoint and cheer our soiled face
With the abundance of thy grace:
Keep far our foes, give peace at home,
Where thou art Guide no ill can come.
Teach us to know the Father, Son,
And thee of both, to be but one;
That through the ages all along,
This may be our endless Song:
Praise to thy eternal merit,
Father, Son, and Holy Spirit.

[Page 168] That done, the Bishop shall pray in this wise, and say,

Let us pray.

ALMIGHTY God and heavenly Father, who of thine infinite love and goodness towards us, hast given to us thy only and most dearly beloved Son Jesus Christ to be our Redeemer, and the Author of everlasting life: who after he had made perfect our redemption by his death, and was ascended into heaven, sent abroad into the world, his Apostles, Prophets, Evangelists, Doctors, and Pastors: by whose labour and ministry he gathered together a great flock in all parts of the world, to set forth the eternal praise of thy holy name : for these so great benefits of thy eternal goodness, and for that thou hast vouchsafed to call these thy servants here present to the same Office and ministry appointed for the salvation of mankind, we render unto thee most hearty thanks, we praise and worship thee: and we humbly beseech thee by the same thy blessed Son, to grant unto all, who either here or elsewhere call upon thy [Page 169] Name, that we may continue to shew ourselves thankful unto thee for these and all other thy benefits; and that we may daily increase and go forward in the knowledge and faith of thee and thy Son, by the Holy Spirit. So that as well by these thy Ministers, as by them over whom they shall be appointed thy Ministers, thy holy Name may be for ever glorified, and thy blessed kingdom enlarged, through the same thy Son Jesus Christ our Lord; who liveth and reigneth with thee in the unity of the same Holy Spirit, world without end. *Amen.*

When this Prayer is done, the Bishop, with the Elders present, shall lay their hands severally upon the head of every one that receiveth the order of Elders: the receivers humbly kneeling upon their knees, and the Bishop saying,

THE Lord pour upon thee the Holy Ghost for the office and work of an Elder in the Church of God, now committed unto thee by the imposition of our hands. And be thou a faithful dispenser of the word of God, and of his holy Sacraments: In the

[Page 170]Name of the Father, and of the Son, and of the Holy Ghost. *Amen.*

Then the Bishop shall deliver to every one of them, kneeling, the Bible into his hand, saying,

TAKE thou authority to preach the Word of God, and to administer the holy Sacraments in the congregation.

Then the Bishop shall say,

MOST merciful Father, we beseech thee to send upon these thy servants thy heavenly blessing, that they may be clothed with righteousness, and thy word spoken by their mouths, may have such success, that it may never be spoken in vain. Grant also that we may have grace to hear and receive what they shall deliver out of thy most holy word, or agreeable to the same, as the means of our salvation; and that in all our words and deeds we may seek thy glory, and the increase of thy kingdom, through Jesus Christ our Lord. *Amen.*

PREVENT us, O Lord, in all our doings, with thy most gracious favour, and further us with thy continual help; that in all our works begun, [Page 171] continued and ended in thee, we may glorify thy holy Name, and finally by thy mercy, obtain everlasting life, through Jesus Christ our Lord. *Amen.*

THE peace of God, which passeth all understanding, keep your hearts and minds in the knowledge and love of God, and of his Son Jesus Christ our Lord; and the blessing of God Almighty, the Father, the Son, and the Holy Ghost, be amongst you, and remain with you always. *Amen.*

* If on the same day the Order of Deacons be given to some, and that of Elders to others; the Deacons shall be first presented, and then the Elders The Collects shall both be used; first, that for Deacons, then that for Elders. The Epistle shall be Ephes. iv. 7, to 13, as before in this office. Immediately after which, they that are to be ordained Deacons shall be examined, and ordained, as is above prescribed. Then one of them having read the Gospel, which shall be St. John x. 1. as before in this office: they that are to be ordained Elders, shall likewise be examined and ordained, as in this office before appointed.

[Page 172] *The Form of Ordaining a Bishop.*

The Collect.

ALMIGHTY God, who by thy Son Jesus Christ, didst give to thy holy Apostles many excellent gifts, and didst charge them to feed thy flock: give grace, we beseech thee, to all the Ministers and Pastors of thy church, that they may diligently preach thy Word, and duly administer the godly Discipline thereof; and grant to the people, that they may obediently follow the same; that all may receive the crown of everlasting glory, through Jesus Christ our Lord. *Amen.*

Then shall be read by one of the Elders,

The Epistle. Acts XX. 17—35.

FROM Miletus Paul sent to Ephesus, and called the Elders of the Church. And when they were come to him, he said unto them, Ye know, from the first day that I came into Asia, after what manner I have been with you at all seasons, serving the Lord with all humility of mind, and with many tears and temptations, [Page 173] which befel me by the lying in wait of the Jews; and how I kept back nothing that was profitable unto you, but have shewed you, and have taught you publicly, and from house to house, testifying both to the Jews, and also to the Greeks, repentance toward God and faith toward our Lord Jesus Christ. And now behold, I go bound in the Spirit unto Jerusalem, not knowing the things that shall befall me there; save that the Holy Ghost witnesseth in every city, saying, That bonds and afflictions abide me. But none of these things move me, neither count I my life dear unto myself, so that I might finish my course with joy, and the ministry which I have received of the Lord Jesus, to testify the Gospel of the grace of God.—And now, behold, I know that ye all, among whom I have gone preaching the kingdom of God, shall see my face no more. Wherefore, I take you to record this day, that I am pure from the blood of all men. For I have not shunned to declare unto you all the counsel of God. Take heed, therefore, unto yourselves, and [Page 174] to all the flock, over the which the Holy Ghost hath made you Overseers, to feed the Church of God, which he hath purchased with his own blood. For, I know this, that after my departing, shall grievous wolves enter in among you, not spaing the flock. Also of your own selves shall men arise, speaking perverse things, to draw away disciples after them. Therefore watch, and remember, that by the space of three years, I ceased not to warn every one night and day, with tears. And now, brethren, I commend you to God, and to the word of his grace, which is able to build you up, and to give you an inheritance among them who are sanctified. I have coveted no man's silver, or gold, or apparel: yea, ye yourselves, know, that these hands have ministered unto my necessities, and to them that were with me. I have shewed you all things, how that so labouring, ye ought to support the weak; and to remember the words of the Lord Jesus, how he said, It is more blessed to give than to receive.

[Page 175]Then another shall read,

The Gospel. St. John xxi. 15—17.

JESUS saith to Simon Peter, Simon, son of Jonas, lovest thou me more than these? He saith unto him, Yea, Lord: thou knowest that I love thee. He saith unto him, Feed my lambs. He saith to him again, the second time, Simon, son of Jonas, lovest thou me? He saith unto him, Yea, Lord: thou knowest that I love thee. He saith unto him, Feed my sheep. He saith unto him the third time, Simon, son of Jonas, lovest thou me? Peter was grieved, because he said unto him the third time, Lovest thou me? And he said unto him, Lord, thou knowest all things: thou knowest that I love thee. Jesus saith unto him, Feed my sheep.

Or this: St. Matt. xxviii. 18—20.

JESUS came and spake unto them. saying, All power is given unto me in heaven and in earth. Go ye therefore, and teach all nations, baptizing them in the name of the Father, and of the Son, and of the Holy Ghost; teaching them to observe all things [Page 176] whatsoever I have commanded you; and lo, I am with you always, even unto the end of the world.

After the Gospel and the Sermon are ended, the elected person shall be presented by two Elders, unto the Bishop, saying,

WE present unto you this holy Man to be ordained a Bishop.

Then the Bishop shall move the congregation present to pray, saying thus to them:

BRETHREN, it is written in the Gospel of Saint Luke, that our Saviour Christ, continued the whole night in prayer, before he did choose and send forth his twelve Apostles. It is written also in the Acts of the Apostles, that the Disciples who were at Antioch, did fast and pray, before they laid hands on Paul and Barnabas, and sent them forth. Let us, therefore, following the example of our Saviour Christ, and his Apostles, first fall to prayer before we admit, and send forth, this person presented to us, to the work, where-unto we trust the Holy Ghost hath called him.

[Page 177]Then shall be said this prayer following:

ALMIGHTY God, giver of all good things, who by thy Holy Spirit hast appointed divers orders of ministers in thy church; mercifully behold this thy servant now called to the work and ministry of a Bishop, and replenish him so with the truth of thy doctrine, and adorn him with innocency of life, that both by word and deed, he may faithfully serve thee in this office, to the glory of thy name, and the edifying and well governing of thy Church, through the merits of our Saviour Jesus Christ, who liveth and reigneth with thee and the Holy Ghost, world without end. *Amen.*

Then the Bishop shall say to him that is to be ordained,

BROTHER, forasmuch as the holy Scripture commands that we should not be hasty in laying on hands, and admitting any person to government in the Church of Christ, which he hath purchased with no less price than the effusion of his own blood; before I admit you to this administration [Page 178] I will examine you on certain articles, to the end that the congregation present may have a trial, and bear witness how you are minded to behave yourself in the church of God.

ARE you persuaded that you are truly called to this ministration, according to the will of our Lord Jesus Christ?

Answ. I am so persuaded.

The Bishop. ARE you persuaded that the holy Scriptures contain sufficiently all doctrine required of necessity for eternal salvation, through faith in Jesus Christ? And are you determined, out of the same holy Scriptures, to instruct the people committed to your charge, and to teach or maintain nothing as required of necessity to eternal salvation, but that which you shall be persuaded may be concluded and proved by the same?

Answ. I am so persuaded, and determined by God's grace.

The Bishop. WILL you then faithfully exercise yourself in the same holy Scriptures, and call upon God, by prayer, for the true understanding [Page 179] of the same, so as you may be able by them to teach and exhort with wholesome doctrine, and to withstand and convince the gainsayers?

Answ. I will so do, by the help of God.

The Bishop. ARE you ready, with faithful diligence, to banish and drive away all erroneous and strange doctrines contrary to God's Word, and both privately and openly to call upon and encourage others to the same?

Answ. I am ready, the Lord being my helper.

The Bishop. WILL you deny all ungodliness and worldly lusts, and live soberly, righteously, and godly, in this present world, that you may shew yourself in all things an example of good works unto others, that the adversary may be ashamed, having nothing to say against you?

Answ. I will so do, the Lord being my helper.

The Bishop. WILL you maintain and set forward, as much as shall lie in you, quietness, love, and peace among all men; and such as shall be unquiet, disobedient, and criminal [Page 180] within your district, correct and punish, according to such authority as you have by God's Word, and as shall be committed unto you?

Answ. I will so do, by the help of God.

The Bishop. WILL you be faithful in ordaining, sending, or laying hands upon others?

Answ. I will so be, by the help of God.

The Bishop. WILL you shew yourself gentle, and be merciful for Christ's sake, to poor and needy people, and to all strangers destitute of help?

Answ. I will so shew myself, by God's help.

Then the Bishop shall say,

ALMIGHTY God, our heavenly Father, who hath given you a good will to do all these things, grant also unto you strength and power to perform the same; that he accomplishing in you the good work which he hath begun, you may be found perfect and irreprehensible at the last day, through Jesus Christ our Lord. *Amen.*

[Page 181]Then shall VENI, CREATOR SPIRITUS, be said.

COME, Holy Ghost, our souls inspire,
And lighten with celestial fire.
Thou the anointing Spirit art,
Who dost thy sev'n-fold gifts impart.
Thy blessed Unction from above
Is comfort, life, and fire of love.
Enable with perpetual light
The dulness of our blinded sight;
Anoint and cheer our soiled face
With the abundance of thy grace:
Keep far our foes, give peace at home,
Where thou art Guide no ill can come.
Teach us to know the Father, Son,
And thee of both, to be but one;
That through the ages all along,

This may be our endless Song:
Praise to thy eternal merit,
Father, Son, and Holy Spirit.

That ended, the Bishop shall say,
Lord hear our prayer.
Answ. And let our cry come unto thee.
The Bishop. Let us pray.

ALMIGHTY God, and most merciful Father, who of thine infinite goodness, hast given thine only and dearly beloved Son Jesus Christ, to [Page 182] be our Redeemer, and the Author of everlasting life, who after that he had made perfect our redemption by his death, and was ascended into heaven, poured down his gifts abundantly upon men, making some Apostles; some Prophets; some Evangelists; some Pastors, and Doctors, to the edifying and making perfect his church; grant, we beseech thee, to this thy servant such grace, that he may evermore be ready to spread abroad thy gospel, the glad tidings of reconciliation with thee, and use the authority given him, not to destruction, but to salvation; not to hurt, but to help; so that as a wise and faithful servant, giving to thy family their portion in due season, he may at last be received into everlasting joy, through Jesus Christ our Lord, who, with thee and the Holy Ghost, liveth and reigneth, One God, world without end. *Amen.*

Then the Bishops and Elders present, shall lay their hands upon the head of the elected person, kneeling before them, upon his knees, the Bishop saying,

RECEIVE the Holy Ghost for the office and work of a Bishop, in the [Page 183] Church of God, now committed unto thee by the imposition of our hands, in the name of the Father, and of the Son, and of the Holy Ghost. *Amen.* And remember, that thou stir up the grace of God which is given thee by this imposition of our hands; for God hath not given us the spirit of fear, but of power, and love, and soberness.

Then the Bishop shall deliver him the Bible, saying,

GIVE heed unto reading, exhortation, and doctrine. Think upon the things contained in this book. Be diligent in them, that the increase coming thereby may be manifest unto all men. Take heed unto thyself, and to thy doctrine; for by so doing thou shalt both safe thyself and them that hear thee. Be to the flock of Christ a shepherd, not a wolf; feed them, devour them not. Hold up the weak, heal the sick, bind up the broken, bring again the outcasts; seek the lost: be so merciful that you may not be too remiss; so minister discipline that you forget not mercy; that when the Chief Shepherd shall appear, you [Page 184] may receive the never fading crown of glory, through Jesus Christ our Lord. *Amen.*

[Then the Bishop shall administer the Lord's Supper; with whom the newly ordained Bishop, and other persons present, shall communicate.]

Immediately before the Benediction, shall be said the following prayers:

MOST merciful Father, we beseech thee to send down upon this thy servant, thy heavenly blessing; and so endue him with thy Holy Spirit, that he, preaching thy word, may not only be earnest to reprove, beseech, and rebuke with all patience and doctrine, but also may be to such as believe, a wholesome example in word, in conversation, in love, in faith, in chastity, and in purity; that faithfully fulfilling his course, at the latter day he may receive the crown of righteousness laid up by the Lord, the righteous Judge, who liveth and reigneth, one God, with the Father and the Holy Ghost, world without end. *Amen.*

PREVENT us, O Lord, in all our doings, with thy most gracious favour, and further us with thy continual help, [Page 185] that in all our works begun, continued and ended in thee, we may glorify thy holy Name; and finally, by thy mercy, obtain everlasting life, through Jesus Christ our Lord. *Amen.*

THE peace of God, which passeth all understanding, keep your hearts and minds in the knowledge and love of God, and of his Son Jesus Christ our Lord; and the blessing of God Almighty, the Father, the Son, and the Holy Ghost be amongst you, and remain with you always. *Amen.*

END OF THE SPIRITUAL PART.

THE TEMPORAL ECONOMY OF THE AFRICAN METHODIST EPISCOPAL CHURCH.

PART II.

SECTION I.

Of the Qualification, Appointment,
and Duty of the Stewards of Circuits.

Quest. 1. WHAT are the qualifications necessary for Stewards?

[Page 186]*Answ.* Let them be men of solid piety, who both know and love the Methodist doctrine and discipline, and of good natural and acquired abilities, to transact the temporal business.

Quest. 2. How are the Stewards to be appointed?

Answ. The preacher, having the charge of the circuit, shall have the right of nomination; but the Quarterly Meeting Conference shall confirm or reject such nomination.

Quest. 3. What are the duties of Stewards?

Answ. To take an exact account of all the money, or other provision collected for the support of preachers in the circuit; to make an accurate return of every expenditure of money, whether to the preachers, the sick or the poor; to seek the needy and distressed, in order to relieve and comfort them; to inform the preachers of any sick or disorderly persons; to tell the preachers what they think wrong in them; to attend the Quarterly Meetings of their circuit; to give advice, if asked, in planning the circuit; to attend committees for the application of [Page 187] money to Churches: to give counsel in matters of arbitration; to provide elements for the Lord's Supper; to write circular letters to the societies in the circuit, to be more liberal, if need be; as also to let them know, when occasion requires, the state of the temporal concerns at the last Quarterly Meeting; to register the marriages and baptisms, and to be subject to the Bishops, the Presiding

Elder of their district, and the Elder, Deacon, and travelling preachers of their circuit.

Quest. 4. What number of Stewards are necessary in each circuit?

Answ. Not less than two, or more than four.

SECTION II.

Of the Salaries of the Ministers and Preachers,
and allowances to their Wives, Widows, and Children.

THIS shall rest with the Annual Conferences respectively.

Every preacher who has the charge of a circuit, shall earnestly recommend to every class or society, in his circuit, to raise quarterly or annual collections. The money received shall [Page 188] be lodged with the Stewards of the circuit, to be brought or sent to the Annual Conferences, with a regular account of the sums raised for this purpose, in the classes or societies, respectively.

SECTION III.

Of raising a general Fund for the propagation of the Gospel.

1. EVERY preacher who has the charge of a circuit, shall make a yearly collection, and if expedient a quarterly one, in every congregation where there is a probability that the people will be willing to contribute: and the money so collected shall be lodged in the hands of the steward or stewards, and brought or sent to the ensuing Annual Conference. To this end, he may read and enlarge upon the following hints:

"How shall we send labourers into those parts where they are most of all wanted? Many are willing to hear but not to bear the expense. Nor can it as yet be expected of them; stay till the word of God has touched their hearts, and then they will gladly provide for them that [Page 189] preach it. Does it not lie upon us, in the mean time, to supply their lack of service? To raise money out of which, from time to time, that expense may be defrayed? By this means those who wilingly offer themselves, may travel through every part, whether there be societies or not, and stay wherever there is a call, without being burdensome to any. Thus may the gospel, in the life and power thereof, be spread from sea to sea. Which of you will not rejoice to throw in your mite to promote this glorious work?

"Besides this, in carrying on so large a work through the continent, there are calls for money in various ways, and we must frequently be at considerable expense, or the work must be at a full stop.

"The money contributed, will be brought to the ensuing Conference."

2. A public collection shall be made at every Annual and every General Conference, for the above purposes.

SECTION IV.

Of the Book Concern.

THE profits of all the Books published by the authority of the General [Page 190] Conference or Convention, shall go to the support of the travelling ministry, as the Annual Conferences from time to time may think proper.

There shall be two book stewards appointed, to conduct the printing and sale of the books. They shall make returns of the money to the treasurer, who shall be appointed by the General Conference or Convention; and after paying the expenses, the treasurer shall forward on the profits of the books to the different Annual Conferences. There shall be an equal dividend made between the said Annual Conferences respectively.

SECTION V.

Of Slavery.

Quest. WHAT shall be done for the extermination of slavery?

Answ. We will not receive any person into our society, as a member, who is a slave-holder; and any who are now members, that have slaves, and refuse to emancipate them after notification being given by the preacher having the charge, shall be excluded.

CONTENTS.

CHAPTER I.

SECTION I. Articles of Religion, 11

SECTION II. Of Justification, 25

SECTION III. Of the General and Yearly Conferences or Conventions, 55

SECTION IV. Of the Election and Consecration of a General Superintendant, and of his duty, 61

SECTION V. Of bringing to Trial, finding guilty, and reproving, suspending, or excluding disorderly persons from society and church privileges, 64

SECTION VI. Of the duty of Elders having the charge, 70

SECTION VII Of the Trial of those who think they are moved by the Holy Ghost to preach, 75

SECTION VIII. Of the Matter and Manner of Preaching, &c. 76

SECTION IX. Of the Duty of Preachers to God, themselves, and one another, 78

SECTION X. Rules by which we should continue, or desist from, preaching, at any place, 82

SECTION XI. Of Visiting from house to house, &c and enforcing Practical Religion, 82

SECTION XII. Of Instruction of Children, 90

SECTION XIII. Of Baptism, 91

SECTION XIV. Of the Lord's Supper, 92

SECTION XV. Of Public Worship, 92

SECTION XVI. Of the Spirit and Truth of Singing, 93

[Page 192]**CHAPTER II.**

> SECTION I. The Nature, Design, and General Rules of the United Societies, 96
> SECTION II. Of Class Meetings, 102
> SECTION III. Of the Band Societies, 105
> SECTION IV. Of the Privileges granted to serious persons who are not of our society, 109
> SECTION V. Of Marriage, 110
> SECTION VI. Of Dress, 111
> *SECTION VII. Of the Sale and use of Spirituous liquors, 112*

CHAPTER III.

> The Order for the Administration of the Lord's Supper, 113
> The Ministration of Baptism of Infants, 124
> The Ministration of Baptism to such as are of Riper Years, 129
> The form of Solemnization of Matrimony, 137
> The order for the burial of the Dead, 145
> The form and manner of making Deacons, 148
> The form and manner of ordaining Elders, 155
> *The form of ordaining Bishops, 172*

PART II.

> SECTION I. Of the qualification, appointment, and duty of the stewards, 185
> SECTION II. Of the Salaries of the Ministers and Preachers, and Allowances to their Wives, Widows, and Children, 187
> SECTION III. Of raising a general fund for the propagation of the Gospel, 188
> SECTION IV. Of the Book Concern, 189
> *SECTION V. Of Slavery, 190*

www.ingramcontent.com/pod-product-compliance
Lightning Source LLC
Chambersburg PA
CBHW020808160426
43192CB00006B/487